RAISING HAPPY CONFIDENT KIDS

Also by Nadim Saad

Happy Confident Me Journal
Happy Confident Me Super Journal
The Working Parents' Guide to Raising Happy and
Confident Children
Kids Don't Come With a Manual
Raising Kids as a Team
Tantrums

Available on Amazon and on **www.happyconfident.com**

RAISING HAPPY CONFIDENT KIDS

NADIM SAAD

First Published in Great Britain by:
Best of Parenting Publishing 2020

ISBN: 978-1-9163870-3-4

Cover Design by Danijela Mijailović
and typesetting Eugene Rijn Saratorio

Set in Minion Pro

Contents

Introduction

As parents, we all want to raise happy and confident children who thrive. And as a Parenting Coach, I was particularly interested in this topic because I have an eldest child who is dyslexic and who struggled academically, and this was affecting her self-esteem and confidence.

But when my middle-child turned eight, she also went through a difficult time, and one day she told me "I hate myself."

This is disheartening for any parent to hear, but for a Parenting Coach who is supposed to be an expert on parent/child relationships, it came as even more of a shock. And particularly because my middle child was doing well academically, and she had always been a very happy kid. I'd noticed she didn't seem like her usual self and had been more sensitive than usual, and she was sometimes being difficult with her siblings, but her strong statement still came as a surprise.

I had a meaningful conversation with her and it turned out that she was feeling this way for two key reasons:

1   She felt 'average,' which is an increasingly common issue for children in our day and age. Although she was doing well academically, several of her friends had 'natural talents'; one was a great gymnast, the other a great ballet dancer, etc.

2   She felt like a 'bad' person because she was being mean to her siblings and sometimes to her friends. She thought her behavior defined her as a person (which is something children often do).

This event moved me so much that I decided to make it my life's purpose to ensure that all children, whatever their character, background or level of confidence, are able to feel happy and confident in their own skin. My aspiration is to empower children so that hearing them say, 'I hate myself' or even 'I feel average' will become a thing of the past.

To achieve this, I realized it was essential for children to develop their metacognition (the awareness and under-standing of their own thinking process) and learn how their thoughts affect their feelings and behavior. So, I created a series of illustrated journals for children called the Happy Confident Me Journals and an online course, with the help of experienced psychotherapists and teachers.

The objective of the journals and the online courses is to explain to children key concepts such as the growth mindset, the importance of positive thinking, mindfulness, etc., and thus enable them to gain a better understanding of the way their mind and emotions work. It also helps them develop key life skills and equips them with a toolkit so they can meet life's challenges head on (see Chapter Seven for a detailed explanation of these life skills and ways to explain them to children).

And as parents, we also need to be able to understand these key concepts and use them to raise our children to be happier and more confident. So I decided to write this book, which draws from the latest research in psychology and neuroscience and shows you how to implement simple, practical steps that will help to develop your children's self-esteem and confidence and maximize their chances of living a happy and fulfilled life.

I discovered many contradictory theories on how to achieve this.

Indeed, for decades, parenting experts seem to have had it all wrong because they believed that you could nurture a child's confidence and self-esteem with superlatives such as 'You're smart', 'Well done' or 'You're amazing'.

This school of thought was at its most popular during the 1990s when it was common practice to give 'participation trophies' so that every child would feel just as 'special' as the others. And these approaches still prevail in some education systems.

Extensive research done in the last 20 years shows that this can be detrimental and even damaging to children.

The challenges of the social media generation

The trouble is that when we repeatedly tell kids 'You're awesome,' 'You're so talented' or 'You're amazing,' if kids perceive themselves to be less than 'amazing,' they are left feeling as though they don't quite measure up. So, rather than raising their sense of self-worth, hyperbolic praise can undermine it.

And when you also take into consideration the fact that children of today are put under intense pressure to strive for success and 'be the best they can be,' it's hardly surprising that many are left feeling inadequate and unworthy when they fall short of such unrealistic cultural expectations.

We see stories every day in the media about the rising rates of anxiety and depression in teenagers and young adults. But even more concerning is that children seem to be having problems with self-image from an increasingly early age. Because when you live in a society where you feel scrutinized and judged, children often become highly critical of themselves and plagued by self-doubt.

On the other hand, for a great many children, their lives are dominated by social media and many spend their spare time competing with friends over who can post the perfect 'selfie.' Some psychologists argue that the implications of this are quite significant because in a relatively short space of time, it appears that children have become more self-centered, entitled and narcissistic.

So, well-intentioned parents who are trying to boost their child's self-esteem can inadvertently end up feeding their child's sense of self-importance and entitlement instead.

Starting in the toddler years, self-centeredness is completely normal and a necessary part of development (see the evolution of self-esteem in Chapter One). But as children grow, this can lead to a sense of entitlement and selfish attitudes as they may start see themselves as the center of the universe.

Although self-esteem is always a good thing, some experts say many parents are raising children to have a sense of superiority, and this sense of superiority, ironically, is rooted in poor self-esteem.

So, trying to instill confidence and self-esteem in our children can be tricky because there's a very fine line between nurturing these characteristics and causing them to develop an inflated sense of their own importance.

So if praising children with 'Good boy' or 'You're so clever' or 'You're amazing' and trying to boost their self-esteem can backfire and undermine children's confidence or end up creating self-centered children, what are we supposed to do as parents to raise children to be happy and confident?

Well, thankfully, the latest parenting research shows that there are effective ways to boost children's self-esteem and confidence and maximize their chances of long-term success, without making them selfish and narcissistic.

This book's objective is to equip you with tools that will help you do exactly that, in order to make your children wiser, more resilient and better able to cope with life's challenges.

What's the difference between self-esteem and confidence?

Self-esteem and confidence are very closely related, and we need a healthy level of both in order to be able to cope with the challenges of life and all of its inevitable 'ups and downs.' Self-esteem is our cognitive and, above all, emotional appraisal of our own worth. More than that, it is the matrix through which we think, feel, and act, and reflects and determines our relation to ourselves, to others, and to the world.[1]

While self-esteem is quite an abstract concept, because it is essentially a reflection of our inner self, confidence is related to action and the way in which we relate or engage with the external world around us. Confidence can be learned and developed; we can become better at something through practice and repetition.

But a high level of confidence alone might not be enough for a person to thrive and particularly to be happy because a person can be confident in one area of their lives and completely unconfident in another. Indeed, it is possible for a person to have high self-confidence and low self-esteem, and a lack of self-esteem can be particularly damaging. Because although a person with a high level of confidence is more likely to seize opportunities and take on new challenges, even if the outcome is successful, if they lack self-esteem they may not feel good about – or reward themselves – for their achievements.

---

[1] Neel Burton M.D., Psychology Today, October 2015 https://www.psychologytoday.com/blog/hide-and-seek/201510/self-confidence-versus-self-esteem

A high level of confidence and self-esteem are both key to being successful in all aspects of life, both personal and professional. They play a massive role in how we think and feel about ourselves and our behavior tends to reflect those thoughts and feelings, whether they happen to be positive or negative.

We start to develop confidence and self-esteem during infancy and this is greatly influenced by our parents' inter-actions with us. For a child to develop a healthy level of both, they need to feel that they are loved by those who are closest to them and have a strong belief in their own capabilities. This allows children to approach new chal-lenges with confidence and better equips them to be able to cope with hurt, disappointment and frustration.

As one would expect, research shows that children with high levels of confidence and self-esteem tend to be more independent and are more likely to perform well at school and grow to become happy and successful adults. They also tend to be 'smarter,' not because they naturally have a higher IQ – which is only one measure of intelligence – than their peers, but because they have developed their EQ (Emotional Intelligence) and have assimilated that their intelligence and abilities can be developed and improved over time. Indeed, other research[2] shows that only approximately 25% of achievement is due to innate intelligence or IQ while the other 75% is attributed to psychological skills (such as persistence, grit, and resilience), which is what this book will focus on.

While self-esteem levels do tend to fluctuate slightly at different stages of a child's development (we will be exploring the various stages of self-esteem in Chapter One) it's important to be able to recognize the signs if your child is lacking confidence in his/her abilities. This could be as a result of some external influence that's outside of your control, or it could be due to a negative experience that your child has had. Whatever the underlying cause may be, children with low self-esteem typically lack confidence in their abilities and have a tendency to 'talk themselves out' of trying new things. This is because they are often so afraid of making mistakes that they tend to avoid taking on new challenges for fear of not being 'good enough'.

One of the stories that really struck me as a perfect example of the potential to develop a growth mindset at any

---

[2] Olszewski-Kubilius, 2013

age, and particularly for a dyslexic child, is that of Dominic O'Brien, eight-time World Memory Champion.[3]

As a child, Dominic O'Brien was diagnosed with dyslexia and was told by a teacher at a young age that he 'would not amount to much in life.' Unsurprisingly, this had a profoundly negative impact upon his self-esteem, and as a result he grew increasingly stressed and reluctant to go to school each day. This wasn't helped by the fact that his teachers were so frustrated with his apathy and apparent lack of effort that they would sometimes literally try to shake him out of his educational stupor.

O'Brien describes how at that time, he felt as though his brain was like a muscle, but that it was in a permanent state of relaxation and in very real danger of atrophy. His situation and feelings towards school didn't improve over the following years, in fact if anything they got worse. The day he left school (at the earliest opportunity) he said it felt at the time, like one of the happiest days of his life. Fast forward to 15 years later and O'Brien went on to perform such an impressive feat of mental agility that it led to him being crowned 'World Memory Champion,' on no less than eight separate occasions.

---

[3] O'Brien, Dominic, *You can have an amazing memory*, 2011, Watkins Publishing

O'Brien's 'memory journey' as he describes it all began in 1987 when he was 30 years old and watching TV. The program featured Creighton Carvello, an accomplished memory man of the time, remembering an arbitrary sequence of 52 playing cards. O'Brien was fascinated – he was so impressed and curious to know how Carvello had achieved this remarkable feat that he sat down with a deck of cards and decided that the best way of working out whether it was possible was by attempting it himself.

With practice, dedication and sustained hard work, he did learn how to memorize that deck of playing cards, and this led to the realization that if he set his mind to something, he could achieve absolutely anything. He gained self-esteem and a level of confidence that he'd never had before, and he describes feeling as though a whole new world of opportunity opened up before him.

O'Brien discovered that there are no limits to where a growth mindset can take you (see definition of Growth Mindset in Chapter Two), and his story demonstrates how intelligence isn't something that we are born with and isn't 'set in stone' as many people believe. It proves that with effort, patience and hard work, even the seemingly most unlikely of people can go on to achieve the most amazing of things.

So one of the key messages that I'd like you to remember as you are reading this book is that you should never lose faith in your child's ability to discover something that will make them feel good about themselves and boost their self-esteem, whatever level they are currently at. Our role as parents is to accompany them on this journey and to simply do our best, and we need to relinquish feelings of guilt if we don't achieve immediate success.

Indeed, some of the recommendations in this book may take a long time to have an effect on your child(ren)'s self-esteem, but they are certainly worth implementing as they can have a significant and positive impact on the quality of their lives.

Thankfully, there are steps that you can take at any age to develop your child's mindset and to unleash their full potential. It starts by becoming more aware of the impact your words and actions have upon the way your child feels about themselves, and that's exactly what this book is designed to help you do.

It will show you how to avoid some of the most common 'parenting traps' such as over-praising and motivating through rewards, and provide you with effective alternatives that will help you develop and nurture your child's confidence and self-esteem and maximize their chances of growing to become happy, successful and resilient adults.

Chapter 1

The Evolution of Self-Esteem in Children

As we discussed in the Introduction, we start to develop confidence and self-esteem during our infant years, and the way in which they both develop largely depends on how our parents interact with us. If children are secure in their connection and relationship with those closest to them (ie. their primary caregiver/s) and have a strong belief in themselves and what they are capable of, these are the foundations upon which confidence and self-esteem are built.

However, as well as generational differences, long-term studies suggest that there are differences between individual children of the same age. So, if a child has low self-esteem compared to the rest of their peers at age six, they are more likely to have comparably low self-esteem at age 10.

So, what does this tell us about how self-esteem develops during our formative years? It tells us that once children have formed a mental image of themselves and how others view them, this informs their thinking, their behavior and their interactions with other people.

In other words, they will start thinking and acting in a way that confirms their original view of themselves, so it becomes a self-fulfilling prophecy. If they expect to be ignored by their peers, they'll be oversensitive to any indication of this. Or conversely, if they expect not to be any good at a new activity, they won't bother trying very hard, and when they get the result they expect, this only serves to further reinforce the negative view they have of themselves.

Typically, children have very high levels of self-esteem when they are young, and it starts to decrease throughout their school years, with significant drops during ages 8-10, and again during the middle of adolescence.

Is it merely coincidence that we see self-esteem decrease in children as they become more focused on themselves and how the rest of the world perceives them?

Children, particularly teenagers, tend to be selfish because as they get older their self-image becomes more complicated. They start to self-analyze and evaluate, which in turn causes them to become more self-critical. As adults, we tend to be more focused on the world around us (family, friends, work, societal issues etc.), whereas when we are in our formative years, our focus tends to be on the 'world within.'

So, what can we as parents do to help? The predominant school of thought in both parenting and education until recently was to try to make kids feel good about themselves by giving them constant praise and unconditional encouragement to try to boost their self-esteem in those tricky formative years.

While it might sound good in theory, the problem with this approach is that it doesn't boost their self-esteem or stop children from being overly self-critical because we can't 'rescue' our kids from this stage of their development. And nor should we want to, because whilst it might be a difficult stage, it is also an essential one.

This isn't to say that we can't support our children through this challenging developmental stage, but there are far more effective ways of doing it than with constant praise, which we will explore later in this book.

But first, let's look at why some children are more prone to having low self-esteem than others in the first place.

Why do some children have lower self-esteem than others?

When our child is struggling with low self-esteem, it's only natural to feel worried, anxious or even guilty. We start to question ourselves: Have I not been supportive enough? Have I been too distant or critical? This leads us to another question – one that psychologists have been (and still are) debating for years: is it nature or nurture?

When relating this question to kids with low self-esteem, the answer is that both nature and nurture play a crucial part in how self-esteem develops throughout a child's formative years.

For example, if a child is born with a tendency to be overactive and lacks focus, and they get negative feedback from their peers and teachers because they struggle to sit still and follow directions, this will impact upon how they perceive themselves, which can then lead to low self-esteem.

Equally, if a child's natural temperament makes them prone to being a perfectionist, and they find that they can't perform as well in an activity as their peers, they may start to feel inadequate and start to compare themselves unfavorably to those around them – this can also lead to low self-esteem.

So, both temperament (nature) and experience (nurture) play an equally important role in the development (or lack thereof) of a child's self-esteem.

How social interactions affect self-perception

Psychologist, Charles Cooley, developed a theory in 1902[4] suggesting that we form our self-image through our interactions with those around us, be they positive or negative.

As parents, we are the people with whom children form their first relationships and experience their first interactions. Therefore, we have a massive influence on how our children view themselves.

Our reactions, be they positive or negative, shapes their self-perception and colors their understanding of themselves, which then goes on to affect their self-esteem as they progress through their formative years. And our

---

4 Cooley, Charles, *Human Nature and the Social Order*, New Brunswick, 1983

influence, and their need for our approval – unlike that of their teachers or peers – endures throughout childhood and adolescence.

As children grow, they start to understand people's expectations and that there are certain standards by which we all must live. The older they get, the more they start to internalize these expectations, and if they find themselves unable to live up to them, this can lead to feelings of guilt, shame and inferiority, which in turn can lead to low self-esteem.

So, it's important to be aware of how we react to our children because the choice between being compassionate or disapproving, amused or angered, can make all the difference to a child's self-esteem, both in the long and short term.

At what age do children start developing self-esteem? Psychologist, Phillipe Rochat, conducted an experiment called 'the mirror test,'[5] which was developed in the 1970s by fellow psychologist, Gordon Gallup Jr., to try to answer this very question.

Rochat took a group of young toddlers (under 18 months) and a group of toddlers (older than 18 months)

---

[5] Rochat, Philippe, *Five Levels of self-awareness as they unfold early in life*, Consciousness and Cognition 2003

and marked all of their noses with a red dot, and then put each toddler in front of a mirror to see what their response would be.

The younger toddlers reached for the reflection of themselves in the mirror as soon as they noticed the dot on their face, while the older group instinctively touched their own nose to rub the red mark off because they were able to recognize that something about the 'self' was different or amiss.

So what does this tell us about their self-esteem? It tells us that kids above the age of 18 months already have some sense of themselves as a person. They understand that they are an 'I' and 'me,' which is why children start using personal pronouns like this between the ages of 18 and 27 months. As any parent can testify, this is also around the time that the 'mine' phase happens for much the same reasons. So, rest reassured that although a lot of parents feel like pulling their hair out at this stage, it's actually a very normal and healthy part of a child's development!

Using the results of the mirror test, Rochat conducted his own research and scoured other developmental studies that looked at how newborns and toddlers interact with mirrors, video recordings and photographs.

As you read the below, please keep in mind that the ages associated with each stage are approximate: every child is different and it's completely normal for children to fall slightly outside these age ranges.

1. Ages 2-4: It's all about me!

"Some scientists consider preschoolers too young to have developed a positive or negative sense about themselves. Our findings suggest that self-esteem, feeling good or bad about yourself, is fundamental, it is a social mindset children bring to school with them, not something they develop in school." Andrew Meltzoff, Psychologist

Typically, kids of this age have high self-esteem. While some children may be a little shy and more hesitant in social situations, the majority crave attention and love an audience to show off to.

Children of this age are only able to view the world through the lens of their own experience, which at this stage of their lives is obviously very limited. They aren't able to evaluate themselves objectively as they haven't yet learned to compare their own abilities with that of their peers. So, as a result of this limited view of themselves and the world around them, they tend to show off their abilities and achievements and make grand claims such as "I'm really fast at running!" or "I can count all the way to 10!".

As we've already touched on, they are also very attuned to the reactions of the adults around them. This is why it's so important to choose your words carefully when talking to children in this sensitive stage of their personal development.

The way a child behaves at this age (or any age for that matter) is a good indication of their levels of self-esteem. However, it's completely normal for all children to go through phases of being shy around their peers or reluctant to take on challenges and explore the world around them. It only becomes a concern if this becomes a regular pattern of behavior.

2. Ages 5-7: Learning new skills and abilities

"We found that as young as five years of age self-esteem is established strongly enough to be measured."
Dario Cvencek

Because kids are learning new skills and improving their abilities at a rapid pace at this age, their self-esteem is often high, due to the fact that they can do things now that they couldn't do a year ago. This fast progression is exciting for kids, and they typically love to share that excitement with others!

They also tend to have a strong focus on fairness, so will look to see how they are being treated compared to their peers and those around them, and if there are any differences they're usually not shy of pointing it out! "That's not fair!", "She's got more chocolate then I have!", and "His toy is bigger than mine!" are words that every parent will have heard at least a dozen times or more.

They are still developing the ability to self-evaluate, so they start to form opinions of themselves based on what others think about them. At this age, they are starting to understand that people judge them based on their actions and their abilities, which is why it's usually around this age that kids start to form ideas of themselves as being talented versus untalented or good or bad at certain activities. This will affect their mindset, as we will see in the following chapter.

Research conducted by Cvencek, Greenwald, and Meltzoff (2016) supports this idea. They conducted a study where they asked a group of five year olds to sort words like 'good,' 'bad,' 'mad' or 'naughty' according to whether the word applied to them or not. So for example, would they describe themselves as being 'nice' or 'mean.'

The findings show that self-esteem is surprisingly strong in children this young, but it also shows that kids' self-esteem can plateau or drop if they see kids doing better at certain activities such as swimming or math, but again this is nothing to worry about as it's a healthy and normal stage of their development.

However, it is around this age that you're likely to see warning signs if a child is going to have issues with their self-esteem. As they start exploring the world around them and trying to understand their place within it, they tend to be rigid thinkers. That's why you'll often hear them say things like "That's for babies!" "Playing with dollies is for girls!". Viewing the world in simple terms makes it easier for young minds to understand, and it also explains why kids of this age tend to have such strong opinions!

Their relationship with their peers at this age is incredibly important and plays a major role in their level of self-esteem. They care deeply about their friendships, but have trouble understanding the true meaning of being a friend because they are still in the process of developing their empathy (and it's a skill that can be developed as we will see in the following chapters). They are still learning how to put themselves in another person's position and imagine how they might feel, which is why you'll find that they may play well with their friends or siblings one minute and then be arguing with them then next. They are also usually very sensitive to criticism or being excluded at this age, especially when that criticism comes from one of their peers.

Kids of this age also have a much better understanding of the past and how their experiences relate and connect to their current situation. They also understand the concept of the future, and will often express dreams of what they hope to become, whether that happens to be a doctor, firefighter, astronaut or scientist.

3. Ages 8-10: Self-critical and judgmental

Issues with self-esteem tend to start at this age because children have developed the ability to realistically compare themselves with others. Having spent more time amongst their peers, they now have the necessary thinking skills to recognize that they are not always the best at what they do, and that some of their peers excel in areas that they do not.

This increased level of self-awareness makes it more likely that a child will adopt a 'fixed mindset' (see Chapter Two) at this age. In fact, statistics suggest at this stage of development, the proportion of children with a 'growth mindset' drops to just 58%.

So, it's not surprising that children of this age tend to view themselves in a more negative light than they did when they were younger, or that the proportion of kids with a fixed mindset continues to increase. This is due to the fact that they have learned to be self-critical and this can lead them to develop a sense of inadequacy.

Suddenly, they become acutely aware of the disparity between who they are and the person they want to be. This is one of the key reasons why children can develop a fixed mindset at this age, which is why it's so important for us as parents to teach them that learning is a process and developing new skills takes time, persistence and practice.

If you hear your child say things like "I'm rubbish at soccer!" or "I'll never be as good at ballet as Amy is!", then this could be an indication that your child has a fixed mindset. They might also be reluctant to try new things or any activity they struggle with, in case it exposes their own perceived lack of 'talent' and ability.

"A major cognitive-developmental advance at this age is the realization that one's self-attributes can be both positive and negative." Susan Harter

During this phase, they understand that they can have both good and bad qualities simultaneously, but if they seem to focus more on their weaknesses than their strengths, this could indicate that they're suffering from low self-esteem. If this is the case, you might notice that they start using coping mechanisms such as putting others down to make themselves feel better, or becoming unreasonably angry when criticized.

Thankfully, there are tools you can use to help raise your child's self-esteem and help them to develop a growth mindset as opposed to a fixed one, all of which we will explore later in this book.

4. Ages 11-13: Appearance is everything

Kids become incredibly self-conscious at this age, and their main focus is on their appearance and their position within the social hierarchy.

The onset of puberty obviously plays a massive part in this stage of a child's development. Bodily changes can increase their feelings of self-consciousness, especially if they don't view themselves as being 'normal' when comparing their bodies with others in their peer group.

Because they are so focused on their appearance and what others think of them, they spend a lot of time looking in the mirror, examining and judging what they look like. And this applies to boys, too. Increasingly, we are seeing boys who are just as 'obsessed' over their appearance and are acutely aware that their bodies don't conform to what they believe to be the 'ideal' male physique.

Due to the fact that kids of this age tend to be highly critical of themselves, they assume that everyone around them is judging them just as harshly. Child psychologist, David Elkind, coined a term for this phenomenon – the 'imaginary audience.' They fear making even minor social mistake, and if/when they do, it can become so magnified in a child's head that to them, it can seem like the end of the world.

To adults, such concerns can seem silly or trivial, but for the child, the emotions they are experiencing are very real indeed, and the opinion of their peers have equally real social consequences.

The reality is, whether we like it or not, kids can be mean, and children of this age are casting judgment on one another all the time. And research suggests that this continues until it peaks at around age 14, while other studies suggest that caring about what others think continues all the way through to our thirties and beyond!

So, while we may think we are being helpful when we tell our kids "It doesn't matter what other people think," we aren't being helpful because to them, others' opinions matter a great deal.

What we can do however, is engage them into 'thinking mode' by asking them questions like "How important is this person, and how much time do you spend with them?" and follow it up with "Do you trust and value their opinion more than your own?". Questions like this help children understand that while everyone they meet throughout their lives will have a different opinion, that's not to say that all of them are accurate or meaningful.

At this age, a child's self-esteem is so dependent on their peers that they can be deeply affected by someone else's view of them. So their moods may oscillate wildly from one extreme to the other because one minute they're feeling like the coolest kid in school, and the next they're a social pariah. Providing them with love, support and understanding during these moments is crucial and can make all the difference to our kids (even if they don't show it!).

Then we also have social media thrown into the mix, which turns out to be a double-edged sword.

On the one hand, it can be reassuring for kids to know that their friends are never far away – they're always available to talk to at the touch of a button. But on the other hand, constant connectivity also means that there are new things to worry about, such as privacy threats and cyberbullying. Where once in the not-too-distant past, a child could shut their bedroom door and not have to worry about school bullies and the like, trying to get most kids to disconnect from the internet is like trying to herd cats – near impossible!

The problem is that social media exacerbates kids' feelings of self-consciousness; it provides a medium that allows them to present a purely positive image of themselves and gives them endless opportunities to compare themselves with others. The 'fear of missing out,' or 'FOMO' as the kids call it, can cause very real distress in some children, as they start to feel that their lives are severely lacking when compared to that of their peers.

While it's understood that frequently checking social media is linked to distress, what isn't known is whether this leads to unhappiness or is a result of children already being unhappy in the first place.

If a child doesn't appear to have a supportive group of friends or is painfully self-conscious to the extent that they are reluctant to spend time with their peers, this could be an indication that that they're struggling and may need some additional help in building their self-esteem.

Another thing to look out for is if online activity starts to replace real face-to-face interactions. Remember, although peer relationships are a child's main focus at this age, their relationship with their parents is equally as important (although their words and behavior might lead you to think otherwise!).

5. Ages 14-16 : Trying to be myself/Who am I?

This is the age when kids start trying to figure out who they really are and tends to be challenging in terms of their self-esteem. During this stage of adolescence, children are usually driven by two things, both of which are in conflict with one another.

On the one hand, they think of themselves as being special and unique, and they seek to distinguish themselves as an individual, so they spend a lot of time focusing on what makes them different. On the other hand, they desperately wish to fit in and be 'part of the gang.' This leaves them in a tricky situation where they are driven by two conflicting needs, so it's no wonder that the stereotypical cry of the teenager is "No one understands me!". How can we hope to understand them, when they are still trying to understand themselves?

Statistics suggest that this is the age where we begin to see dramatic differences in depression rates between the genders. Although it's completely normal for teens of both sexes to be quiet and moody, when this behavior is constant and they exhibit it when around both their parents and their peers, this could be a sign of concern.

Depression tends to be more commonplace in girls of this age, but that's not to say that boys aren't at risk as well. Sadness, anxiety, irritability, changes in appetite or sleep patterns, and losing interest in their favorite activities are all possible red flags, which could perhaps point to depression.

But thankfully, there are steps you can take and tools you can implement that will help you find solutions to these challenges, all of which we are going to explore over the course of this book.

Chapter 2

The Importance of Mindset

"Our studies show that teaching people to have a 'growth mindset,' which encourages a focus on effort rather than on intelligence or talent, helps make them into high achievers in school and in life."

Carol S. Dweck

Professor at Stanford and Author of

'Mindset The psychology of success'

Recent research has made significant discoveries in the understanding of what makes children want to take on challenges and why they can become afraid of mistakes. And consequently, the effect this can have on their confidence, self-esteem and level of resilience.

For many years, psychologist Carol Dweck[6], and her team at Columbia and Stanford examined a group of primary school children and focused on how they

---

[6] Carol Dweck - Mindset

responded to praise. She discovered that children tend toward one of two mindsets.

The first is a 'fixed mindset,' when a child believes that his or her intelligence is 'set in stone' and will therefore only choose tasks that they deem appropriate to this level of intelligence, lest they risk failure. The second, healthier mindset is the 'growth mindset,' belonging to the child who is happy to take on new challenges because they see them as opportunities for growth and new experience, even if this involves making mistakes.

Dweck discovered that a child's experience of praise had a direct influence over which of these mindsets children were more likely to adopt. The first group of 'failure-fearing' children were generally used to being praised for their intelligence with words such as 'you're smart/clever,' whereas the second group possessed more of a 'try and try again' attitude and were more familiar with being praised for their effort rather than the outcome.

As Carol Dweck explains, "Emphasizing effort gives a child a variable that they can control. They come to see themselves as in control of their success. Emphasizing natural intelligence takes it out of the child's control, and it provides no good recipe for responding to a failure."

1. The implications of a fixed mindset in children

People with a fixed mindset believe that their basic level of intelligence, skill and ability is 'fixed' from birth and therefore can't be developed or improved over time. So when a child has a fixed mindset, this can affect everything from their attitude to learning and education right through to their willingness to take on new challenges or try new things.

Children are unlikely to take part in an activity, whether it be a sport or something educational, if they don't believe they can develop their ability and get better at it over time. They are far more likely to stick with the things that they are good at in the belief that that is where their 'natural' abilities lie. Because if they attempt something new and don't get it 'right' first time, then this could serve as proof that they lack intelligence. And as we touched on earlier in the Introduction, once a child starts to question their level of intelligence and/or abilities, this can have a damaging effect on their confidence and self-esteem.

Evaluative praise is closely linked to causing children to have a fixed mindset – this is because evaluative praise 'grades' children according to their perceived level of ability. For example, if we tell children they are smart, they may feel that they have to live up to this perception all the time and will start to avoid anything that may call their level of intelligence into question, for fear of disappointing us. As a result, they may start to develop an aversion to some things that they find more difficult, and it can lead to them disliking, and therefore avoiding, these 'harder' things in the long-term.

As explained, a mindset is a set of personal beliefs and is a way of thinking that influences our behavior and attitude toward ourselves and others, which explains why there is such a close link between a child's mindset and their level of confidence and self-esteem.

However, whilst it's important to be aware of the differences between a growth mindset and a fixed mindset, it's equally important to avoid categorizing children as possessing either one or the other. We have to remember that people rarely fit neatly into one category; we all display certain characteristics of each mindset depending on our mood and the situation.

2. Neuroplasticity is a key discovery

Are you different to the person you were fifteen years ago? Of course you are! This is because our brains are shaped by our experiences, which is why the way we think and behave now is different from when we were younger.

This constant fluctuation and the way in which our brains adapt over time, is called neuroplasticity. Each new thought, emotion or interaction creates a new neural pathway in the brain, and as we repeat those behaviors, the neural pathway is reinforced and becomes stronger.

Neuroplasticity enables us to learn new skills, and get better at them over time. Much like a muscle in the body will get stronger through repeated use, the brain gets 'stronger' in the exact same way. Performing a thought or behavior over and over again increases its power, until it becomes automatic.

So how does this relate to a child's mindset? Neuroplasticity is key to understanding the concept of mindset. As we discussed in the sections above, someone with a fixed mindset will give up if they find something too challenging, whereas those with a growth mindset understand that through practice and repetition we can learn to do almost anything. And this is at the very heart of why the principles of neuroplasticity are so effective in helping to improve childrens' physical and mental ability and raising their confidence and self-esteem.

So, neuroplasticity is essentially the 'muscle building' part of the brain, in a very literal sense, we become what we think and do.

And what's fascinating about the human brain is that once we learn these skills and the associated neural pathways have been forged in the brain, we don't forget. The pathways may become weaker if we don't use them (just as they become stronger with frequent use), but they never disappear entirely. So there's truth in the old saying, 'you never forget to ride a bike!'

Neuroplasticity happens throughout our lives. However, unsurprisingly our brains adapt more easily when we're young. As we get older, the brain loses some of its plasticity, which is why we usually become more fixed in our opinions, as well as in the way that we think and behave.

Through understanding the principles of neuroplasticity, we can teach our children how to improve their skills, increase their ability to take on new challenges and utilize their brainpower to maximum effect.

Because when children have a better understanding of the way in which their brains work, this helps to bolster their self-belief and equips them with the tools they need to try new things, embrace their mistakes and unlock their full potential.

3. The evolution of mindset in children

What is quite surprising is how the mindset of children evolves according to their age. Research shows that in Kindergarten, 100% of children have a growth mindset, but this decreases to 58% once they reach Grade 3!

Here are the changes in mindset across school years (research from *'Mindsets in the Classroom,'* by M.C. Ricci, 2013):

School Year	Fixed Mindset	Growth Mindset
Kindergarten	N/A	100%
Grade 1	10%	90%
Grade 2	18%	82%
Grade 3	42%	58%

What explains this big increase in fixed mindsets in children is that with every increase in year, more students start to believe that their intelligence is a fixed trait. They start incorporating the notion that 'some people are smart and some people are not.' This notion becomes stronger as children start encountering more challenges and having more tests and are subsequently graded according to their academic 'ability.' This explains the significant jump in children who develop a fixed mindset between grades 2 and 3.

This shows that the earlier we work on developing a growth mindset in children, the better! Once this mindset is ingrained, it is still possible to change it, but it requires more time and effort.

Assessing children's mindset

In order to help children develop a growth mindset, it is useful to assess their current mindset[7]. To achieve this, you can use simple questions that can be adapted to specific situations, because while children may have a growth mindset and believe that they can influence the outcome for some activities, they may have a completely fixed mindset when it comes to other things.

Your child's answers to the questions below will help to give you a better indication of whether he/she has a fixed or a growth mindset:

- Do you think that everyone can learn new things?

- Do you think that some kids are born smarter than others?

---

[7] Cay Ricci, Mary and Lee, Margaret, *Mindsets for Parents*, 2016, Prufrock Press Inc

- Do you think that we can actually change how smart we are?

Most children are likely to agree with the first question, and answer that all of us can learn. However, this is not enough to define a growth mindset, as it is their answers to the following questions that will help you determine whether your child believes that their intelligence is fixed or whether they can improve it, the latter being the basis of the growth mindset.

If your child seems to display a fixed mindset, you should try implementing some of the recommendations in this book and reassess your child with similar questions after a month or so. Their mindset will hopefully have changed by then and they'll be convinced that they can increase their intelligence and achieve many things if they put in enough effort and practice.

4. Developing a growth mindset in children

What Dweck's and other neuroscientific research such as neuroplasticity shows is that the brain is like a muscle – it gets stronger with use. When we communicate this same message to our children and we focus our praise on things that they can control, the effect on their attitude and ability to learn is astonishing.

Helping kids to understand that the struggles we experience when we are learning new and challenging things are normal and are actually a sign of neural connections strengthening in our brains, is a powerful way to transform their attitude and their perspective. Increase of motivation, willingness to accept new challenges, and healthier reactions to failure are only a few of the benefits children experience when they understand how their brains work (See Chapter Seven for ways to explain these concepts to kids).

The real life example of Dominic O'Brien, eight-time World Memory Champion in the Introduction is a great testament to this. Once kids have a better understanding of how their brains work, this boosts their sense of autonomy, which leads them to put more hard work and effort into their studies. They become naturally curious and are intrinsically motivated to problem-solve and acquire new knowledge and skills through sustained effort and hard work. And it also bolsters their love of education, meaning that they are always looking to learn more.

So, by equipping children with the skills and knowledge they need to understand how their brains work, we are maximizing their chances of developing a lifelong love of learning and education.

5. Relation between self-esteem and confidence and mindset

As one would expect, research shows that children who have a growth mindset have higher levels of confidence and self-esteem, tend to be more independent and are more likely to perform well at school, all of which increases their chances of unlocking their potential and growing to become happy and successful adults.

They also tend to be 'smarter,' not because they naturally have a higher IQ – which is only one measure of intelligence – than their peers, but because they have developed their EQ (Emotional Intelligence) and have assimilated that their intelligence and abilities can be developed and improved over time.

Conversely, a child with a fixed mindset believes that their skills and intelligence are 'set in stone,' so they are less likely to try new things, which only serves to further reinforce the negative view they have of themselves.

So, this tells us that self-esteem and a child's mindset are closely linked. Dweck's research into praise suggests that the most effective way of raising your child's self-esteem and nurturing confidence is by first assessing their current attitude toward skills, learning and intelligence, and then equipping them with the tools they need to develop a growth mindset.

Children with a growth mindset believe that perseverance and effort are the key to success, so they have the confidence to take on new challenges, without worrying about 'failing' or getting everything right first time.

In fact, kids with a growth mindset don't view making mistakes as having failed at all, they see them as an opportunity to improve and grow.

Thankfully, as parents we can influence our children's mindset through the way we react and interact with them, and therefore maximize their chances of having healthy levels of self-esteem as they progress through childhood and adolescence and into adult life.

And considering that mistakes are an inevitable part of being human, in helping our kids develop a growth mindset, we are equipping them with one of the most important skills of all – the ability to cope with anything that life throws their way. And that's exactly what we're going to do over the course of this book.

Chapter 3

Typical Parenting Mistakes that Affect Children's Self-Esteem

"You can't let praise or criticism get to you. It's a weakness to get caught up in either one."
John Wooden

Every parent wants to boost their children's self-esteem and confidence. However, the latest research shows that some of the things that parents do with the best of intentions can actually be detrimental to a child's self-esteem, particularly because our actions can make children doubt our sincerity and cause them to become afraid of failure.

Given the research on fixed and growth mindset, you can probably already imagine some of these typical parenting mistakes.

Here are the five most common mistakes that most parents make:

1. Using evaluative praise

One of the keys to developing a child's self-esteem is to make them feel good about themselves, and many parents think that the best way of doing this is by ensuring that children receive lots of praise and encouragement. And whilst it is true that some forms of praise and positive comments made to our children are likely to motivate them, research shows that certain types of praise can actually do more harm than good.

Indeed, research suggests that using evaluative praise with statements such as "You're smart" or "You're good at this" can create a fear of failure, because children become afraid to do anything that could expose their 'flaws' and call into question their 'talent.'[8]

And yet such praise is commonly used by parents because it used to be advised by parenting experts in the 'self-esteem building culture' of the last couple of decades. Using such evaluative phrases focuses on our children's 'innate' talents rather than their ability to develop new skills, and we run the risk of boxing them into adopting a certain identity. Because if a child identifies as being 'smart' or 'good,' they may feel as though they have to live up to

---

[8] Carol Dweck - *Mindset*

that perception all the time, and this pressure can lead to children becoming afraid of failure.

Such pressure results in children becoming less likely to try new things or take risks for fear of not getting it 'right,' and so they end up missing out on essential opportunities to develop their confidence and sense of self. They are also likely to start disregarding their parents' appreciation of them because they grow to become cynical of this praise and may doubt its sincerity.

Rather than making children feel better about themselves, evaluative praise often has the opposite effect, in that it can cause them to focus on their weaknesses. For example, if we tell our child that they are an excellent reader, their reaction might be, "How can I be an excellent reader? It took me twice as long to finish the book than all the other kids in my class." It can also lead to feelings of immediate denial and disbelief: "I don't know why they're praising my drawing when the one I did yesterday was so much better – they're just saying this to make me feel good." Or in some cases, it can even be experienced as manipulation: "I haven't done anything to deserve the praise they're giving me, they must only be saying it because they want something from me."

Even though we may use it with the best of intentions, evaluative praise puts too much pressure on children to live up to our idealized perception of their ability and 'talents' and often serves only to make children feel uncomfortable. Indeed, many parents find that the more praise they try to give as their child grows up, the quicker their child is to reject it!

That's not to say that we should avoid praising our children altogether, in fact quite the opposite is true. The key is to praise in a more effective way in order to develop a growth mindset, as we will explore in the following chapters.

2. Focusing on the outcome

If we tend to focus on the outcome by praising them with statements such as: "I'm so proud of you for getting 100% in your school test," we can inadvertently overlook the effort that our children have put in on the occasions when they don't excel or aren't successful in an exam or activity. As we will see in the following chapters, the effort they put into something and the potential mistakes that they make when they don't get it 'right' are usually more valuable experiences for developing self-esteem than the outcome itself.

Also, if we only praise our children if they achieve a good outcome, then we run the risk of making them feel as though they have to 'win' or be successful every time, and if they don't achieve it then they are somehow failing. For some children, this feeling can make them afraid to take on new challenges. This fear is often driven by the worry that they will disappoint us if they fail to excel, so they start to avoid situations and challenges that may expose them as lacking in ability.

It can also cause children to think that if they don't reach the desired outcome (scoring highly in a test, winning a soccer match etc.) then they won't receive their parent's praise. And for many children, this apparent withholding of praise can feel like a criticism.

3. Criticizing and comparing to others

There is nothing more demotivating for a child than receiving a constant 'diet' of corrective feedback or 'constructive criticism.'[9] This can make them feel singled out and as if they're being shamed for aspects of their personality or behavior.

And yet, it is quite easy to find ourselves as parents in 'error detection' or 'fault-finding' mode, particularly when we feel our child is being lazy and is not putting enough effort into a task or activity. This is particularly true when

---

[9] Fay, Charles, *Love and Logic Finding your Children's Gifts*

it comes to exams and grades. It is tempting to look at an exam and point out all the mistakes and this is particularly demotivating for children.

When we focus on highlighting what the child has done well instead, it boosts their confidence and makes them believe that they are capable and that they will be able to improve. When we do need to provide feedback, it's important that we try to do it in a way that will not affect their confidence. (See Chapter Four for more ideas on how to do this.)

It is also essential that we avoid comparing them to a better-behaved sibling or school friend as this is also demotivating, and it could send children the message that they have innate flaws and therefore have little to no capacity to change.

4. Overpraising and going overboard

Giving children constant praise for even the slightest of achievements may seem like a good way of increasing their confidence, helping them to become more competent and improving behavior. This type of constant 'positive reinforcement' is still advocated by a lot of parenting experts nowadays. However, research shows that praising children indiscriminately means that our praise is likely to become meaningless to them and loses its power to influence over time.[10]

By being praised for everything they do, children are likely to become 'praise junkies' and to be overly influenced by what other people think of them because they are so used to being evaluated. This also makes it more likely that they will become 'people-pleasers' as adults who seek constant validation from other people. As a result, they may find themselves frequently being either 'made' or 'broken' by someone else's opinion of them.

Similarly, if we become over-excited when praising children for the slightest of achievements, this can make them doubt our sincerity. In other words, if we go too 'over the top,' we may find that in the long term our children become cynical of our praise and start to doubt the sincerity of the appreciation we have for them.

Another issue is that if we repeatedly tell kids "You're awesome," "You're so talented" or "You're amazing," if kids perceive themselves to be less than 'amazing,' they are left feeling as though they don't quite measure up. So, rather than raising their self-esteem, hyperbolic praise only serves to undermine it.

---

[10] Henderlong and Lepper, *The Effects of Praise*, 20021

Children are very good at sensing when we are not being authentic in our interactions with them, so if we do this too often we may find that it starts to negatively impact upon the trust and connection we have with them.

This is especially true of older children; while young children will tend to accept what we say without question, teenagers are usually more aware of the possible motives behind our words and actions. With maturity comes a certain level of cynicism as well as the ability to question, so keep this in mind when praising older children.

And as we touched on earlier, the other problem with exaggerated praise is that children of today are already under such intense pressure to look perfect and be perfect, that if they perceive themselves to be less than this, this can leave them feeling emotionally crushed.

And when you also take into consideration the conflicting messages kids get about who they are and what they should be from their friends, parents, teachers and social media, is it any wonder that so many end up with a distorted view of themselves?

The way that children react to these pressures differs from child to child. Some children respond by pushing themselves harder to try to prove their worth. This can result in them putting all their focus and effort into pleasing others, even though it doesn't make them truly happy, and then giving up in anxiety and frustration. While other kids adopt a mentality of 'Why bother? I'm only going to fail miserably and embarrass myself' and decide that the safest thing to do is stop trying altogether.

But the one thing that many of today's children have in common is that going overboard with praise has caused them to have an unhealthy preoccupation with self-worth.

5. Using reward systems and sticker charts

Rewards and sticker chart systems have become hugely popular over recent years; parents use them as a means to encourage good behavior from their children and help them develop a positive attitude towards daily tasks and household chores.

Whilst such systems can certainly be effective in the short term, the reward chart system teaches kids that the only point in being well-behaved is that they will be rewarded for it. Indeed, research shows that the external motivation provided by the reward becomes stronger than the internal motivation of simply behaving the way they should.[11] This means that if we constantly reward our children for something now, we are effectively reducing the chance for them to repeat that behavior again unless they are cajoled with more rewards.

This can be difficult for some parents to accept, as rewards and sticker charts often tend to produce quick and impressive results. However, the change in behavior is unlikely to last because such reward systems only focus on increasing the external motivation of the child, rather than having any real effect on their beliefs or attitude. This is because rewards don't encourage children to think about or take responsibility for their behavior, don't help to teach them 'right from wrong' and nor do they have any influence upon their moral development.

They are essentially a way of 'bribing' our children to do as we ask and once we remove the reward, the good behavior disappears with it. In the long term, parents are very likely to find that their children come to expect greater and greater rewards so that by the time they become teenagers, they may refuse to comply with any of our requests without some form of reward such as a financial incentive.

---

[11] Warneken and Tomasello - *Extrinsic rewards undermine altruistic tendencies in 20-month-olds* - Dev Psychol. 2008 Nov

You do most of the above? You're in the right place!

If you're used to making some or all of the mistakes listed above, which are very common, this book's objective is to equip you with more effective ways of praising that will help to raise your child's level of self-esteem and maximize their chances of growing to become confident and independent adults.

Chapter 4

How to Talk to Children and Praise Them to Develop Self-Esteem and a Growth Mindset

"If parents want to give their children a gift, the best thing they can do is to teach them to love challenges, be intrigued by mistakes, enjoy effort, and keep on learning. That way, their children don't have to be slaves of praise. They will have a lifelong way to build and repair their own confidence…"

Carol S. Dweck

Professor at Stanford and Author of

'Mindset The psychology of success'

As we've touched on previously, research has shown that the way we speak to our children, and particularly the way we praise them, has a significant impact not only on their willingness to learn and take on challenges in life, but subsequently on their self-esteem and their behavior as a whole. This is because children naturally crave their parents' acceptance and appreciation, so the way we interact with them, including the nature of the comments that we make, directly influences the way they feel about themselves.

We therefore need to be more conscious and aware of how we talk to our kids, and learn how to praise them in a way that develops their self-esteem and growth mindset, rather than undermines it.

1. Being Specific

As we discussed in the last chapter, it is important not to 'over-praise' our children with general statements such as "This is great!" or "You're so clever!", because as soon as they spot that we are so hopelessly biased that we will admire just about everything they do, our praise can become meaningless. Our children start to doubt the sincerity of our praise, and in the long term our words of appreciation can backfire by causing children to develop a fixed mindset.

Instead of praising our children with general/evaluative words, it is more effective to acknowledge their effort, behavior or even their attitude. Praising specific aspects of their achievement in this way will help them learn to self-evaluate their abilities in the future. So, for example, Dweck's research shows that telling your child "You've done really well, you must have put a lot of effort in this" is much more effective than yet another "You've done well, you're really smart."

Often, just describing something that your child has achieved, or expressing interest in the achievement by asking a question about how they did it, is the best way to praise a child. So for example saying, "I really like the way you mixed the colors in your picture" is better than "That's a lovely picture."

2. Praise the effort, the persistence and the progress

It's important that we praise our children only for the traits that they have the power to change. When we focus on a child's effort and progress, rather than their achievements or level of ability, we encourage them to learn the art of motivation as we help them to recognize that sometimes tasks require us to put in effort over a long period of time. We want them to think, "Yes, I worked really hard to get to this result, so it's worth making the effort in the future." Encouraging them to adopt this attitude will also make them less afraid of making mistakes as they start to recognize that they are an essential part of the learning process.

So rather than praising our children for getting a high grade or winning at a game or sports match, it's much more effective to praise them for the effort they have put in:

- For example, "I can see by how you're playing the piano how much you must have practiced."

- Or "You know your times tables by heart, I can see that you've put a lot of effort into learning them."

- Or alternatively, we can ask them to explain the reason for their success, as it will usually be the effort/practice they've put into it e.g. "Why do you think you were able to achieve such a good score on your spelling test?".

3. Praise descriptively and describe the 'process'

It is easy to fall into the 'over-praise' trap, and this often depends on our culture or the way we were raised. If you tend to praise your children a lot, it's important not to feel guilty about it and totally rein in your natural tendencies. Instead, you can improve the *way* you praise by praising descriptively and describing the process (as opposed to evaluative praise as explained in Chapter Three).

Focus on strategy and the process of learning rather than the outcome, and praise the steps a child takes as this shows them that each step is a necessary part of achieving something. Our child(ren) will appreciate that we have taken an interest in their work and how it was executed, and they'll be more likely to realize their achievements and want to share them with us in future.

- For example, instead of saying, "Wow, this is so beautiful!" try asking them a question, "How did you do this part?".

- Or describe what we see, "Wow the chicken in your drawing looks so lifelike!".

- Instead of "I'm so proud of you for getting a good grade in your exam!" try, "You must be so proud of yourself for all the effort you put into revising for your exam."

- Avoid statements such as "That picture is amazing – you're going to be the next Picasso!" and replace with "The picture you've drawn is so lifelike – it must have taken you a lot of time to add in all that detail."

4. Always be honest and praise specific actions rather than their overall behavior

Praise everything our children do and they will either discount what we are saying, or become dependent on praise for self-affirmation. So, it's important to avoid praising children if they do something that they're supposed to do. For example, when they carry something to the table or throw their shirt in the laundry, a simple "Thank you" is sufficient.

Even young kids can see right through false praise, so it is important to remain honest. That said, some people have a tendency to 'under-praise' in fear that doing the opposite might 'spoil' their child. Be aware that this is not good either, as children do need our encouragement and positive comments to feel good about what they do.

When we do praise our children, it's important to focus on a child's specific actions rather than their overall behavior, as this enables children to realize that their behavior is something they choose rather than something they are. And once they start to understand that they have control over how they behave, this empowers them to be able to make better choices in future.

- For example, instead of saying, "You behaved really well when Granny was here" we can say, "I really appreciated that you helped Granny get in and out of her chair during her visit."

- Or, rather than, "You were so good at the grocery store today" try "Thank you for carrying the shopping basket at the grocery store today, it was really helpful."

- Instead of "You were really well-behaved at the dinner table tonight, you're such a good boy" try "Your table manners at dinner today were excellent – I really appreciate the effort you made because it makes dinnertime so much more enjoyable for everyone."

- Avoid statements such as "I'm so proud of you for being such a good boy at swimming class today" and replace with "You must be so proud of yourself for the effort you made at swim class today. I could see that you were really concentrating on every word the teacher was saying."

Also, 'staged' eavesdropping – for example praising children to a partner or another adult within their hearing – can also be a great way to acknowledge a child's specific actions.

- For example, you could say, "Have you noticed how helpful Kirstie has been recently? Her room is always tidy, and I never have to ask her to do her chores, she just goes ahead and does them. I love that she's maturing into such a kind and responsible girl."

- Or, "Did I tell you how well Peter is doing in English? He's been putting so much time and effort into his homework recently, and the teacher said that he's been making some excellent contributions in class. And he's even reading for fun in his spare time! It's great to see that he's enjoying it so much."

5. Make it about them

One of the keys to self-esteem is to have a realistic view of ourselves and self-evaluation is crucial in achieving this. What we ultimately want is for our children to develop their own power of self-evaluation and self-awareness.

Without a healthy level of self-awareness, children can become 'praise junkies' who are dependent on us to tell them if they are doing well. They can develop a kind of 'false self,' which they adopt and adapt to please the adults around them, or to get what they need from the world. Therefore, our aim as parents is to nurture a child's ability to self-evaluate and help them acknowledge their own achievements.

When we feel proud of our children, it's only natural for us to want to tell them so and we may express this by saying, "I'm so proud of you." But this innocuous sentence makes it 'about us' rather than them without our even realizing it.

The problem is that when we keep telling our kids how proud we are of them, it can make them feel pressured to live up to our high expectations. And then suddenly every achievement they make becomes about keeping us happy, rather than taking part in a task or activity because they are intrinsically motivated to do so.

When we show our children that we notice what they do and that we are particularly interested in their opinion of how they did it, it enables them to self-evaluate in future rather than become dependent on our opinion or judgment.

Here are some examples that will help you praise your children in a way that makes it about them, so they don't start depending on you or other people to acknowledge and validate their achievements

Instead of saying, "I'm so proud of you" try asking them, "You've worked hard and did well on this test, are you proud of yourself?". And once they answer, "Yes I am," you can always add: "I'm proud of you too!".

Instead of, "You haven't studied enough for this test, which is why you had a mediocre grade" try "Are you happy with this result?".

Most children are actually more demanding of themselves than we'd expect (particularly when you apply the techniques in this book!), so they will usually answer: "No, I'm not happy with this, I could've done better." And you can encourage them to find strategies/solutions that would work for them by asking "So what can you do to improve this next time?". This will empower them to apply the strategies they come up with, which could simply be "studying more!"

6. Accentuate the positive and focus on the strategy

It's important that we try to ensure that our positives outweigh the negatives so that we fill our children's 'I'm capable' account instead of filling their 'I'm not capable' account.

There is research that estimates that children need at least three times more positive comments than negative ones in order to be motivated and confident.

To achieve this, focus on their uniqueness rather than on their weaknesses, reduce criticism and start by always identifying the good things in something that your child has done (be it a test, homework, a drawing, etc.) before speaking about potential improvements.

To help them understand the strategies that have worked for them (ie. things that they can control!), ask them to explain the reason for their success and the steps they took along the way. These steps will usually involve practice and effort, but it can also be a different way of learning something, or the help that they've sought from someone, or who they did something with, etc.

If you feel that there is room for improvement, allow them to self-evaluate (see above), so you can simply add: "Are you happy with the result" or "What could you better next time?". And if you have a tendency to say, "No, that's not the way to do this," try making a suggestion instead: "I see that you've done it this way. There's another way of doing it that you might prefer, shall I show it to you?".

Finally, when a child's predictions or comments are overly negative, our role is not to counter their gloom with false predictions or unreasonable expectations, but to teach them not to undermine their confidence with self-defeating and fixed mindset talk. So instead of offering basic reassurances to 'look on the bright side,' encourage them to think about specific ways to improve a situation and bring them closer to their goals.

7. Get rid of the 'but'

When encouraging your child to self-evaluate, and particularly if you feel there is room for improvement, you should ideally address what could be improved separately from the conversation on what is positive (if at all possible). So for example, try not to use the typical sentence: 'It sounds like you're happy with this, BUT what can you do to improve this further?", otherwise, your child will most certainly hear 'It's good, BUT it's not good enough.'

Even we adults will tend to hear the same when someone tells us that we did something well and they add a "BUT!" We will all have a tendency to disregard what comes before the 'but' and only focus on the negative part of the sentence. This mindset can stay with kids for the rest of their lives, and it explains why many adults suffer from the 'I'm not good enough' syndrome.

By making the two conversations, and therefore the two subjects, separate, we avoid undermining their confidence, which enables them to focus on what they can do to improve things, rather than worrying about not being good enough.

8. Real life example – Encouraging self-evaluation and developing a growth mindset

When our daughter Noor was five years old, we started discovering all the amazing research described in this book and we learned the importance of encouraging our children to self-evaluate. This meant that we no longer just focused on our own feelings about our children, but instead we made a conscious effort to start allowing our children to express their feelings towards us and what was happening to them. So we started changing our language and instead of saying "I'm so proud of you," we replaced it with "You've been putting in so much practice and effort, you must be really proud of yourself." Our daughter's response to this was invariably: "Not really, it was easy," whatever the activity.

Six months into trying this, we were starting to really wonder if this was working with our daughter and we started doubting the effect this new language was having. But shortly after that, she came home one day from ballet and exclaimed "I am so proud of myself because I was named ballerina of the month!". We didn't immediately answer (which would've done in the past!), but instead looked at her with an approving smile and this gave her time to add: "And it's all because I've been practicing really hard!". This was exactly what we had hoped for all along – not only did she feel proud of herself, which clearly improved her self-esteem and confidence, but she also understood that all the effort and hard work she had put in had enabled her to achieve this.

A few months later, we took Noor to see 'Cirque du Soleil' for the first time, and she was mesmerized by the circus performers. About 10 minutes into the show, she turned to us and said, "Wow, they must have put in so much practice to be able to do that?!". We were so pleased that she had reached this conclusion by herself; she was demonstrating that she perfectly understood what it meant to have a growth mindset and could see for herself how much practice is required to excel at something.

However, by the time Noor turned seven, we realized that although Noor had incorporated a growth mindset with regards to activities such as ballet, gymnastics, swimming and tennis and some academic subjects such as math, she had actually developed a fixed mindset with regards to reading and writing.

She had been struggling with her reading over the last school year, and slowly but surely started to fall behind. We knew that she was struggling, but didn't worry about it too much as we recognized that all children develop at different rates, and we trusted in the education system to support her and encourage her in the areas in which she was having difficulty. We also recognized that there are countries where they delay reading until a later age, so perhaps she simply wasn't 'ready.'

We also felt that if we swooped in and tried to fix the problem, we'd blow the situation out of all proportion and probably make Noor dislike reading even more. The last thing we wanted was for her to carry her dislike of reading into adulthood. We were stuck in quite a tricky situation, feeling unsure as to what was the right thing to do. The problem was that her reluctance to read was getting worse. Not only was she struggling with the basics, but she also became really anxious when doing it and even when talking about it, especially when sitting down to read with me.

Neither of us could really understand what was making her so anxious and over the next few months, despite our best efforts to encourage her, the problem snowballed until it actually prevented her from getting into the school we had wanted. This was our 'wake-up call,' as it was clear by now that the problem wasn't going to rectify itself, and it wasn't just a phase that Noor was going through. In fact, it was getting worse, so now was the time for us to act.

We sat down and talked about how we had dealt with the situation thus far, and we realized that we could do a lot more to help Noor to develop a growth mindset about reading. Although we'd encouraged her to practice her reading and made time to read with her, we hadn't really been consistent enough for her to make some steady prog- ress, which is essential in her feeling more confident and developing more competence.

We also thought about what could be making Noor so anxious when reading with me, and realized that up to now, my impatience for her to improve had made her afraid to read with me in case she made mistakes. In order for Noor to feel more comfortable reading with me, I first had to make her feel better about herself and make her feel that mistakes are ok. I had to lower my expectations and make an effort to be more patient and empathetic with her struggle.

We decided that the best way to approach the situation was to sit down with Noor and involve her in the process of creating a reading program that we would implement over the summer break. Involving her in this way was a great way of encouraging her to open up and share some of the problems she had been experiencing. Plus, we knew that if she had a say in creating the schedule, she'd be far more likely to stick to it.

By taking the time to listen to Noor and showing more empathy for her struggle, we soon discovered that she was feeling frustrated at the fact that she wasn't able to keep up with kids her own age. We also learned that her teacher had made her afraid of reading and making mistakes because she had sometimes shown some frustration at Noor's slow pace (as I had also done at home!).

So over the summer break, we implemented this strategy. It didn't all go smoothly – there were quite a few power struggles along the way! But with our help and encouragement, which focused on the effort and progress she was making, Noor soon realized that the more she practiced her reading, the better she got. This growth mindset didn't happen overnight, it took sustained effort, but the results couldn't have been any better.

After a couple of months of regular practice, we sat down the Sunday before starting school for a family meeting (see Chapter Six) and – as we do at the beginning of each of these meetings – we shared gratitude and compliments with one another. Noor amazed us by coming up with a new initiative – she asked "Can I be grateful for myself?". "Do you mean that you want to share something that you're proud of?" we asked. "Yes! I am proud that I have finished 'Charlie and the Chocolate Factory' and that I am reading much better now, and I am enjoying it more!" she nodded excitedly. We were absolutely beaming! We thought that her idea of sharing what she is proud of during a family meeting was great and we now implement this – we ask each and every member of the family what has made them feel proud every week.

What made this situation even more valuable is that we discovered after this episode that Noor was actually dyslexic and had a problem with her eyes that prevented her from reading 'normally'! As a result, Noor began doing daily exercises to correct this eye problem and started wearing glasses to read, which made her progress even faster.

And so the moral of this story became even clearer: we need to focus on building a growth mindset in our children, and this cannot be developed by us simply having high expectations of them. By showing our children that their struggles and mistakes are 'normal' and being truly accepting of them, while at the same time praising their effort, progress and persistence, we encourage them to take on new challenges and make them unafraid to make mistakes.

Conversely, if our children become afraid of making mistakes because they see our frustration when they are not learning as fast as we'd expect them to, then we can run the risk of completely demotivating them and causing them to develop a fixed mindset.

Chapter 5

Developing Self-Responsibility and Resilience

"All the adversity I've had in my life, all the troubles and obstacles, have strengthened me. You may not realize it when it happens, but a kick in the teeth may be the best thing in the world for you."
Walt Disney

Our ultimate goal as parents should be to develop our children's self-responsibility and resilience, as these are the key factors that help to boost their confidence and self-esteem and enable our kids to stand strong on their own two feet.

Self-responsibility is the realization that we are the author of our choices and actions. Developing self-responsibility means coaching children to find solutions to their own problems, rather than growing up expecting to have their problems solved by others.

Resilience is the ability to persevere when things get tough and to bounce back from difficult situations.

A significant part of our role is the ability to let go so we can teach our children to be independent and meet the challenges of adulthood. Once a child is able to use their 'thinking' head to solve their problems, they are well positioned to understand and appreciate their own role in events – including what they are responsible for and what they aren't.

When we give our children responsibility, whether it's the responsibility to complete a task on their own or find the solution to a problem, we are showing them that we trust them. And when we show that we trust in them, they find it much easier to start trusting and believing in themselves.

With this self-belief comes a sense of power and competency, which is key to building a child's confidence and self-esteem, and the following tools will show you how you can build on that sense of empowerment, both in the short and longer term.

1. Help them discover their individuality

Self-esteem comes from feeling good about ourselves and understanding what we're good at and ultimately what makes us unique. The most effective way of achieving long-lasting change in a child's level of confidence and behavior is by increasing their internal motivation. When children engage in a behavior or activity purely for the enjoyment of it, they do so because it is intrinsically rewarding and not because they are trying to earn an external reward (see Chapter Three for why it's important to avoid external rewards).

The first step is to help them identify their unique skills. When they are young and lack experience, it's important that we allow our children to experiment with different activities so they can find things they enjoy and that they 'naturally' have more facility/aptitude at. This will help them enjoy the process of learning and improving, and they will be less likely to give up in the face of difficulty because they enjoy the activity.

As they grow, we can help them make a list of their skills. However, it's important not to make children feel that skills are innate – the idea is to make them feel that they have control over the outcomes and to not 'box them in,' because it's normal for children to have more facility/aptitude at some things than others. It's good for them to recognize this and to develop these abilities, while being careful to ensure they don't develop the feeling that they're not good at other things.

So for example, you could sit down with them and make a list of what they really enjoy and what they find easy: e.g. being good at a sport (soccer, gymnastics, dancing, etc.), playing a musical instrument, or having some specific traits that come naturally to them. For example, they may possess traits such as being a 'helper,' a 'caregiver,' etc. Although this may sound like 'boxing in' or labeling children, research shows that expressing these characteristics as a trait increases the likelihood of them adopting this trait.

A great forum in which to do this is a Family Meeting (see Chapter Six). The key is to ensure that we highlight their skills in a way that doesn't sound like evaluative praise and doesn't focus on their innate character. The idea is to make children feel that they have the opportunity to develop the abilities and characteristics that make them unique.

2. Develop perseverance and resilience by finding things that will challenge them

Self-esteem also comes from struggle and overcoming adversity. It's important that our children don't only do things that come easily to them and find (age-appropriate) challenges that they can overcome. Encouraging children to find their own solutions to problems significantly increases their confidence because it helps them to realize that they can overcome difficulties without relying on another's intervention or praise. The brain has to learn to persevere through challenges.[12]

It is therefore essential to allow children to struggle when facing challenges as this gives them the opportunity to develop perseverance, grit and resilience, which are key skills to develop overall resilience in life.

When they encounter challenges, rather than 'saving them' by intervening, we can help them by suggesting alternative strategies to achieve what they are trying to do. You should start by giving your child empathy for their difficulty or feeling (e.g. "You seem to have really struggled with your math homework; math can be tricky sometimes.") Then you can help them find strategies to make things less challenging, such as 'chunking' things, i.e. dividing a bigger challenge into smaller parts to make it more achievable.

As explained in Chapters One and Two, up until around the age of four or five, most children have a growth mindset because they find the majority of things they do to be pretty easy. Of course, there will still be occasions when they put effort into a task or activity, but when children are very young they tend not to be aware of this.

---

[12] Bronson, Po and Merryman, Ashley, *Nurture Shock*, Ebury Press, 2009

However, this doesn't mean that we shouldn't praise them for the effort that they've made. Because although they may not understand immediately, if we continue to praise them for their perseverance and effort, over time they will begin to see that there is a direct link between how much effort they put into something and what they are able to achieve.

As children grow, they will start to encounter more challenges, some of which they will inevitably struggle with. As adults, it's easy to forget just how much you're expected to learn when you're a child, and even easier to forget the frustrations that go hand in hand with learning new skills.

Best-selling author, Tim Ferriss, uses the following graph to illustrate the highs and lows of trying to acquire a new skill. His example refers to learning a new language, but the same principles can be applied to learning practically any new skill.

This graph is really useful for children as it provides a visual representation of the challenges that they are likely to encounter when trying to learn something new. When children know what to expect, they can better prepare themselves for the emotions they are likely to experience and are far less likely to become overwhelmed by them.

Confidence/Fluency

You do it well

Understanding the
basics

It feels harder

You feel the
difference

It feels easier

You feel
rewarded

You want
to give up

Perseverance
Resilience
Confidence

Time

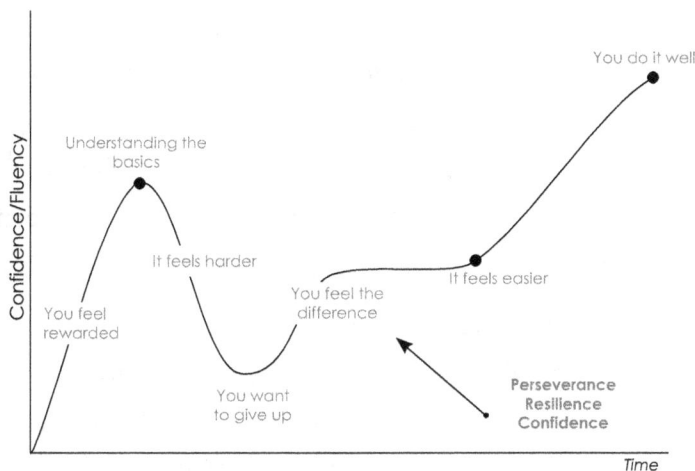

Adapted from Tim Ferris – The 4 hour Chef

What this chart means

When we try our hand at a new skill or activity, generally speaking there will be an initial period of accelerated
learning. We usually take on more information and learn
quickly when we are just starting out at something and this
tends to make us feel more confident, and this is no less
true for children.

Once the learner has grasped the basics of a new sport,
language or skill, learning starts to become more challenging because the beginner is expected to move beyond
the basics and towards the more complex aspects of their
chosen subject or activity. It is usually at this point that the
person realizes that they aren't progressing as quickly as

they were before. This almost invariably dents their confidence and negatively impacts upon their motivation to want to continue learning because their belief in themselves has decreased. It is at this point that many children (and adults!) decide to give up what they had set out to learn because it becomes 'too difficult.'

If the person perseveres in spite of this, the brain will start to adapt whatever it is they are learning to make it easier to process and create new neural pathways (see Neuroplasticity in Chapter Two), essentially allowing the brain to do less to achieve the same outcome. Some people refer to this phenomenon as muscle memory or habit formation. If we refer to the graph, we see that it is at this point that the speed of learning hits a plateau – the person is still making an effort to learn and they may still have low morale due to the fact that they are not learning as quickly as they did in the beginning.

When people persevere, they will eventually reach an 'inflection point,' and it is at this stage where something 'clicks' and learning suddenly becomes easier. This increased ease of learning enables the learner to become proficient at the task or skill in question if they continue practicing. This is a key point where perseverance leads to increased resilience and confidence.

This graph is particularly useful for children (and adults!) because it enables them to anticipate, and therefore prepare for, the emotions they are likely to experience and the difficulties they are likely to encounter, which makes it less likely that they will give up during their most challenging moments.

What we can do as parents is that when children express frustration during a challenge and say something like "I'm no good at this" is remind them about this learning curve, and the fact that they are not *yet* good at something, but that it will get easier if they persevere because their brain will build new neural pathways. 'Yet' is a powerful word and is the epitome of a growth mindset vs. a fixed one, because it reminds children that this is a temporary state and they can improve things with effort.

3. Celebrate Mistakes and Challenges

To develop a growth mindset and resilience, children need to feel that it's normal and important to encounter challenges and make mistakes as ultimately they can learn from them. One way to do this is to help them understand that FAIL can be thought of as a 'First Attempt In Learning' and that taking action and failing would yield less regret than failing to try in the first place.

The other primary cause of children developing a fixed mindset is a child's interpretation of, and their attitude towards, the mistakes that they make. Making mistakes is a part of being human, so if our children are afraid of making them, they will be less likely to take on new challenges and will be very resistant to doing anything that is unfamiliar, which is hardly a good preparation for the realities of adult life.

As Carol Dweck explains, "Many parents react to their children's mistakes as though they are problematic or harmful, rather than helpful. In these cases, their children develop more of a fixed mindset."

It's important to recognize that our attitude as parents has a significant influence as to whether our children are able to learn from their mistakes or become afraid of making them. So when our kids do make mistakes (which they inevitably will!), we must try to resist the urge to intervene and 'rescue' them. Of course, it's only natural that as parents, we want to protect our children from getting hurt, feeling discouraged, or making mistakes of any kind. We love them so much that we can't bear to see them suffer, so we frequently find ourselves swooping in and 'rescuing' them from challenging situations.

Whilst we may have the best of intentions, when we intervene too much in their activities, we often rob our children of the opportunity to learn the invaluable lessons that making mistakes and the process of trial and error has to teach.

It can also cause children to become anxious if we keep issuing them with warnings about life's dangers. And phrases such as "I told you so" only serve to distance them further away from taking responsibility for their mistake and/or learning from its natural consequences, and it also makes children less inclined to listen to what we have to say.

"It's particularly important for young children to have the chance to play and take risks without feeling that their parents will criticize or correct them for doing something wrong."[13]

Every childhood experience, if handled well, can become an invaluable learning experience. Allowing our children to make mistakes and experience their natural consequences teaches them that it's ok to get things wrong from time to time, and as a result they will become better equipped, not only at handling their mistakes, but also at preventing them in the long term.

It's important to have faith in our children and believe that they can survive upset, frustration and disappointment

---

[13] Kathy Hirsh-Pasek, PhD, professor of psychology at Temple University, Philadelphia

because they will become more confident and resilient in the process. So for example, when trying to get them invited to a birthday party they weren't included in, or pressuring the soccer coach to give them more game time, we're not doing them any favors because we're removing valuable opportunities for our kids to develop their 'disappointment' muscle. Kids need to know that it's ok to fail, and that it's normal to feel sad, anxious, or angry. They learn to succeed by overcoming obstacles, not by having us remove them.

So what we should try to do instead, however hard it may be, is start learning to identify which mistakes we need to allow our children to make. Such mistakes are known as 'affordable' mistakes (as opposed to 'unaffordable' mistakes that could result in serious upset or injury), and by allowing our children to deal with the 'natural', i.e. the immediate and logical consequences of their mistakes, means that they become much better at recovering from the upset of mistakes and finding ways to solve them in the long term.

4. Lead by example

As explained in the previous section, it's clear that our attitude as parents has a significant influence upon whether our children learn from their mistakes or become afraid of making them and ultimately on their overall mindset. So it's important that we show our children how to embrace their mistakes by modeling this behavior when we make a mistake ourselves.

For children to develop a growth mindset, it's crucial that we set the right example because children typically imitate their parents and their mindset. So it's important that we demonstrate our growth mindset to our children as often as possible, and try to catch ourselves when we are not modeling the best example.

Ideally, we should find as many opportunities as possible to demonstrate a positive attitude, and show our children that even during tough times we're always going to strive to adopt the 'glass half full' perspective. By adopting this attitude, we are demonstrating to our children that there are positives to be found in any mistake or challenge.

If we have a tendency to use negative language "I'm not any good at this" or "This is so difficult," we should try to replace them with more growth-oriented statements:

- For example, "I'm not as good as I'd like to be at this, I need to practice more."

- Or "I haven't yet mastered this, it requires a lot of effort, but I know that it'll be worth it in the end."

- Instead of, "This is difficult, I don't know why I'm bothering!" try "This is turning out to be quite the challenge, but I know I'll get there in the end if I keep at it."

- Avoid using statements such as "This is so frustrating – I'm never going to be any good at it!", and replace with "It may be challenging right now, but I know that if I put enough time and practice into it, I'll get better soon."

And when something doesn't work out as we expected:

- Instead of, "I can't believe I made this mistake, I'm really stupid!" try "It's completely normal for me to make mistakes in the early stages, but I don't mind because I know that this is all part of the learning process."

- Avoid using statements like, "I completely messed this up" and replace with "Although I didn't get it right this time, I really learned a lot from the process and I can't wait to give it another go."

5. Give them a sense of control

When we order people to do things, we are making an assumption that they are incapable of making the decision for themselves, so it's not surprising that their reaction is usually negative because we are sending them the message that we don't trust them. This also applies to children and even though they don't seem to be responsible enough to make many choices, there are much better alternatives to ordering them around that will boost their confidence and self-esteem, rather than undermine it.

Even kids as young as two are able to consider the consequences of their decisions. Every decision we make in life is a choice, and it is therefore essential to allow children to make decisions early on so that they are able to learn from these choices. When kids make their own (age-appropriate) choices, they feel more in control over their lives and more confident, and our role as parents is therefore to teach our children to make choices from as early an age as possible.

Various internet sources estimate that an adult makes about 35,000 remotely conscious decisions each day, and in contrast a child makes about 3,000[14]. We need to learn to make effective choices when we are young, and learn to bear the consequences without feeling down because we made a choice that we consider to be a mistake.

However, giving children open choices can create anxiety and delay decision-making, so the best replacement for orders/commands is to offer them Limited Choices.

---

[14] Sahakian & Labuzetta, 2013

By offering children limited choices (that suit us!), we can empower them to think for themselves and give them a sense of autonomy, which means that they also become more responsible for their actions.

- For example, rather than "Put on your coat, we're leaving now" try "Would you like to put your coat now or once you're outside?".

- Instead of "We're leaving in five minutes" try "Would you like to leave now or in five minutes?".

These seemingly unimportant choices make all the difference to your children by making them much more cooperative and boosting their self-confidence.

As children grow, you can start giving them more complex choices, but it's still important to also offer some simple choices. Even offering simple choices makes a huge difference when we incorporate it into our daily lives because it significantly reduces the number of orders and commands that we have to give our children.

6. Ask questions

We tend to repeat ourselves a lot when we order our children around, which amounts to nagging and reminding. The intention of asking questions is to replace ordering, nagging or reminding our children to do something with questions. The idea is to put our children into 'thinking mode' by asking them, in an empathic voice, what they think they should do next or what the solution might be to a specific problem.

It is important to make sure that we are engaging our children's attention; when they have their 'thinking hats' on, they are far less likely to be confrontational. So for example, rather than telling them what they're supposed to do, it is better to ask respectfully and without accusation or sarcasm: "What are you supposed to do now?".

Asking questions, instead of using nagging and reminding, encourages children to think about their actions, decisions or intentions and put them into context. It makes them much more likely to answer and comply than they would have been were we to have ordered them around. This type of thinking acts as an invaluable blueprint for future decisions. The more children are able to learn to question and then work out their own behavior, the better equipped they are to be self-disciplined and responsible later in life when we're not around.

If you've made your expectations clear and have already told a child a few times that they are supposed to do something, instead of reminding them or correcting them, you can use this tool in the following circumstances:

- For Routines, e.g, putting things away, brushing teeth, taking a bath, preparing for an activity, etc.

    "What are you supposed to do with your school bag?"

    "What are you supposed to do next?"

    "What do you need to put in your bag to go swimming?"

- To develop good habits:

    "What do we say when we receive a gift?" instead of "Say thank you."

- When children are not behaving appropriately:

    If your child is misbehaving (for example, they have invited a friend over and they are not following the house rules), simply ask "How do we usually do that in this house?"

- When children are asking you for something they know they can't have:

    If your child asks you: "Can I have an ice cream" when it's 30 minutes until dinner, try responding with another question: "What do you think?" or if they tend to answer "Yes" try "What time do we have an ice cream or sweets?".

- When children make a mistake:

If a child needs to be corrected (for example, if they spill a drink), rather than resorting to blame and nagging simply ask: "What could you do about this?"

More often than not, they will already know how to deal with the situation and will clean up the mess. Your job is to encourage them to reach this point by engaging their attention and getting them to think for themselves.

When children are still a little confused or unsure as to what to do next, they may benefit from a bit of coaching, so try asking them, "Do you want some ideas as to what you could do about this situation?".

You can also use Asking Questions to help your children open up and share:

- Parents often ask their children "How was school today?" with genuine interest, but will receive a typical answer of "Ok." Thankfully, there are much more effective questions that you can ask your children to help them open up:

   "What was your best moment at school today?" (Or "What was your worst moment at school today?")

   "What did you learn today?"

   "When were you happiest today?"

"What part of the day do you look forward to? What part of the day do you dread?"

Once they start speaking, it's essential that you allow them to speak freely and refrain from judgment. If they share something that's bothering them, resist the urge to intervene and try to fix things for them. Instead, use Empathy and Validation (see Chapter Six). This will make them want to share even more in future.

7. Problem Solve

As parents, we may often tend to skip straight to offering solutions to our children when they present us with a problem, or to implementing consequences or punishment when they make a mistake. This doesn't give them the opportunity to solve their own issues or to participate in finding solutions to improve their behavior. In doing so, we are not empowering them to find solutions to these problems for themselves, and we are not giving them opportunities to develop their confidence and self-esteem.

When we choose to intervene because our child has encountered a problem of some kind, we are invariably doing it with the best of intentions. Unfortunately, rather than protecting our kids we are actually robbing them of an invaluable opportunity to find solutions for themselves. Seeing our children struggle with any kind of problem can be difficult, but when they learn to deal with it themselves, this encourages critical thinking and helps to increase their levels of resilience and self-esteem. So that when they do encounter problems in the future, they will have confidence in their ability to cope.

Problem Solving becomes one of the most used tools once children are four or older because it is the most effective in empowering children to find solutions to the problems they bring back home.

It is also the most effective at dealing with misbehavior as it involves children in finding solutions to problems that occur in the wider family rather than focusing on consequences and punishment, which can have detrimental effects on motivation.

We can even involve children in setting rules, choosing logical consequences and by asking them how they would prefer to be reminded should a misbehavior occur. This is a great way of teaching children to think for themselves and encourages them to be responsible for their own actions, which makes it far more effective than any other form of discipline.

How to Problem Solve

This tool can be used in two different ways:

1. **When *your child* has a problem, which they tell you about** – for example, they have no friends, they don't like an activity anymore such as Thomas' example below, or they are struggling to do their homework on time (which by the way is their problem, not yours!):

   a) **Encourage your child to take ownership of their problem by asking them, "What could YOU do about this?"**. The answer to this question is usually, "I don't know," particularly if they've not been 'coached' to find solutions to their own problems before. So you can respond to this by saying, "Do you want me to help give you some ideas to start with?" or "Would you like me to tell you what some other children have tried?".

   b) If they say, "No thank you," say, **"Ok, but if you change your mind, I'm always here to listen."**

   c) If they say, "Yes please," **give them some different options of possible solutions.** Offer them at least two solutions.

d) **Empower**: After you explain each solution, encourage your child to evaluate it by asking, "How would that work for you?". If you can't come up with any ideas straight away, simply say to your child, "Let me have a think about it and check how other kids have dealt with this problem, and I'll get back to you."

e) **Show interest, but avoid interfering**: Once your child has decided on which solution they think would be the most appropriate course of action (either one that you have suggested or one they have come up with themselves), all you need to say is, "Let me know how it all works out – good luck!".

2. **When *you* have a problem that you want to discuss with your child**: Perhaps you would like your child to improve a certain aspect of their behavior and you want to involve your child in finding solutions to this issue:

a) **Initiate a problem-solving session**: The most effective way of doing this is by doing some-thing that your child enjoys or alternatively, you can incorporate this session into a family meeting. Identify exactly what the issue is without blaming your child for the behavior, while explaining why this doesn't work for you.

b) **Ask your child questions that show that you're in it together**: "What could WE do about this?"

c) **Work together with your child to generate what possible solutions there may be to the problem in question**. Talk about what you could both do differently next time the problem presents itself.

d) **Listen to their suggestions carefully, asking them**: "And how do you think that would work for you?"

e) **Have a brainstorming session**: Decide on what you each think are the best solutions and then brainstorm together about how you could implement them.

f) **Ask your child how they would prefer to be reminded should they break your agreement**: If they don't have any ideas of their own, help them come up with a fun way to remind them.

8. Real life example – What to do when children encounter challenges

The following scenario is one that most parents experience with their children at some point or another. As parents, we want our children to be as active and constructive with their time as possible, so we try to schedule in many activities for them – and sometimes too many. The problem is that in our desire for our children to learn new things, acquire new skills and be productive with their time, we can actually cause them to develop a dislike of or in many cases, even a fear of learning.

The graph earlier in this chapter is a great way of illustrating this point as it shows us that it's totally natural for children to find some stages of the learning process more difficult than others. Our job is to try to let our children know that it's ok to find things difficult sometimes and that it's totally natural to hit a plateau when trying to learn a new skill. It's important to remember that how we react to our children's challenging moments will have a huge impact on their attitude towards learning, and will play a major role in determining whether they are willing to try new things and whether they give up in the face of challenge and difficulty.

Thomas (10) is having a conversation with his parents about going to soccer practice. The parts between brackets and in italics are what Thomas is thinking as he listens to his parents:

Scenario A: *What not to do*

"I don't want to go to soccer practice anymore, it's boring." Thomas tells his parents.

"But Thomas, you used to enjoy soccer practice so much?! Surely this is just a phase, and you'll probably love it again next time you go?"

(*As usual, you don't hear me and you're just trying to make me change my mind. Can you not see that I am really struggling with soccer practice at the moment? It's become so hard and I'll never be any good at it!*)

Thomas answers: "Nothing, I just don't want to do it anymore."

His parents look at him, somewhat surprised by this admission and ask "But what about the game on Saturday, don't you want to show everyone how good you are and get a permanent position on the team?".

(*Why are they saying this to me when it clearly isn't true?*)

"And how will you ever get to be a soccer player if you don't go to practice?"

"But I'm not any good at soccer, I'm nowhere near as good as the other boys, and I don't want everyone to laugh at me if I get it wrong. Soccer practice is much too hard, so I've decided that I don't want to be a soccer player anymore," he replies and crosses his arms over his chest.

His parents immediately swoop in with reassurances:

"You're such a natural when it comes to soccer though, Thomas, you'd be wasting so much talent if you gave it up!"

Thomas frowns in disbelief at his parents' words of encouragement.

(*So I'm supposed to have been born with a talent to play soccer? How am I supposed to believe them if they just keep telling me how brilliant I am at everything?! I don't actually believe that I have any talent at all as it's proving to be so hard, so I may as well just give up now.*)

Thomas leaves the room and leaves his parents disappointed at not having been able to change his mind, as they really wanted him to continue soccer because they thought it was important for him in life.

Scenario B: *How to effectively deal with these types of situation*

"I don't want to do soccer anymore, it's boring." Thomas tells his parents.

"You're now finding soccer boring?"

"Yes, it's boring and it's hard."

"You're finding it hard? We're guessing that all the stress around the game on Saturday and how much practice you have to put into this probably hasn't helped?"

('How did they guess that I am freaking out at the idea of the game?')

"Yeah… I'm not sure I'm any good at soccer as I'm finding it really hard."

"It sounds like you're finding it hard, but as you know, in this family we don't give up just because something is too hard – so what could *you* do about this?"

"I dunno," Thomas shrugs.

"What if we told you that the way you're feeling is completely normal?"

"What do you mean?"

"Well, when we start a new activity we all go through what's called a learning curve. At first the activity seems really easy, and we tend to get really good really quickly, which makes us feel good about ourselves. But after a little bit of time, we hit a bit of a wall and start to feel that we're not learning as quickly anymore."

"And what happens then?" Thomas asks.

"Well, then we have two choices, we can either give up or we can choose to stick at it. If we give up, then we'll be less likely to want to try new activities in future because we'll just figure that unless we have a natural talent at it, then it'll be too hard so what's the use in trying.

But if accept that making mistakes and not getting things right first time is all part of the learning process, then we'll soon discover that with time, effort and practice, we can achieve just about anything."

"Really? So even though I'm not as good as the other boys right now, I could be if I practice hard enough?"

"Exactly! The best soccer players didn't get there overnight, and they don't become accomplished because they were born with a natural talent. They probably spend more time practicing each week than you spend going to school! They got to be as good as they are because they knew that if they set their mind to it, and put in enough effort and practice, they could achieve pretty much anything they wanted to."

"Wow!", Thomas exclaims and before his parents can say another word, he runs off to his bedroom. Seconds later he comes back downstairs with his soccer shoes on and a huge grin on his face: "Can I practice soccer in the garden before dinner please? I want to make sure that I'm prepared for the big match on Saturday."

"Of course you can! I guess that means that you want to continue with soccer after all then?"

"I sure do! How else am I going to be a professional soccer player when I'm older if I don't go to practice?", he responds and happily runs to the garden to practice.

Scenario analysis:

In the first scenario (A), Thomas felt dismissed by his parents, and then felt that they were trying to reassure him without really paying attention to how he felt or what he had to say. And they focused on innate talent, which is something that he has no control over.

In scenario B, the key is that his parents didn't give him an opportunity to start any 'negative self-talk,' as they first focused on connecting with him by using empathy (see tool in Chapter Six). This meant that Thomas felt listened to.

They then asked Thomas what *he* could do about the way that he was feeling, so they made him realize that this was his problem and not theirs, but clarified that in their family, people don't quit just because something is hard. They then offered him suggestions, rather than swooping in with reassurances. The explanations and solutions they offered gave Thomas a growth mindset perspective on his difficulties, and this is the mindset that really helps children make sense of things.

Although this scenario may sound idealistic, it often happens this way if we allow our child to express their feelings, let go of the negative feelings and then help them replace these negative emotions with growth mindset strategies. If Thomas had still reacted negatively and left the room saying that he wanted to stop playing soccer, the empathy displayed by the parents and the growth mindset perspective would give them the opportunity to revisit this conversation with Thomas later on, where they could offer him other suggestions to ensure that he continues trying. And if this approach doesn't work, and as long as the parents have tried growth mindset strategies, then they may have to accept that their child might want to focus on another activity.

Chapter 6

Connection as the Foundation of Your Child's Self-Esteem

"I define connection as the energy that exists between people when they feel seen, heard, and valued; when they can give and receive without judgment; and when they derive sustenance and strength from the relationship."
Brené Brown

As we explored earlier in the book, establishing a strong emotional bond with our children is crucial to building their confidence and self-esteem, as is having a good relationship with their peers.

Connecting with children on an emotional level also vastly increases the likelihood of them cooperating with us and wanting to do as we ask. Because when we appeal to the right side of their brain – the part of the brain responsible for feelings – their emotional needs feel met, and they are much more capable of redirecting their emotions and/ or behavior.

For a child to feel really confident about their parents' love, they need to feel that our love is unconditional, which can be challenging because when we feel that our children are misbehaving and express our discontent with anger or other 'strong' reactions, they can often interpret this disapproval or disappointment as a withdrawal of our love, and this perceived withdrawal can negatively impact on their self-esteem.

It is therefore important that we try to understand the reasons for their behavior by listening and validating our children's feelings and using empathy in order to connect with them. Connecting with our children in this way will help them learn how to deal with unpleasant or challenging emotions so that they grow to trust themselves and their reactions in the long term, which is a very important foundation for self-esteem. It will also help them learn how to self-regulate their emotions, making misbehavior much less likely in future.

Here are a set of tools that will help you connect with your child at a deep level to ensure they feel unconditionally loved and secure in their relationship with you, which will increase their chances of developing a healthy level self-esteem and confidence.

1. Spend one-on-one time

To create a strong emotional bond with our child, we need to spend time with them. This has become more difficult nowadays, particularly in families where both parents are working. Often, we cannot increase the time that we spend with our children, and we therefore need to make sure that we make the most of this time spent together.

This is particularly important to keep in mind for dads, as they generally spend less time with their children than moms.

One-on-one Time is a key way of building a long-lasting connection between us and each of our children, 'filling-up their emotional bank account' and raising their self-esteem and confidence. One-on-one Time is distinct from ordinary 'ad-hoc' time spent together in that it has to be scheduled and anticipated. And because it is designated one-to-one time, we need to make efforts to keep the rest of the world at bay, including other family members while this special time is taking place. The idea is that special time, far from feeling forced or artificial, delivers what it promises – in other words, it becomes an island of special, focused bonding time between parent and child.

Why it works

Most (if not all!) of our children's 'mis'behaviors are a call for us to give them significance and connection. And when we give a child One-on-one Time, it goes a long way to satisfying their basic need for attention, which can significantly reduce their need to confront us or enter into a power struggle.

Because One-on-one Time exists as a focused island of time spent between the two of you, it is a period of peace, togetherness and communication, which you can both look forward to throughout the rest of the week. Above all, it allows parent and child to get to know each other in a peaceful and caring fashion.

How to give One-on-one Time

- At the beginning of a day or a week, schedule some time that you can dedicate to each of your children individually.

- For children younger than five, try to schedule at least 10 minutes every day. With children older than five, you can do it less regularly, but for longer periods. You should ideally schedule at least 30 minutes once a week.

- Tell your child at the start of your session, "This is our One-on-one Time together."

- Offer a choice of two or three activities to do together (all of which appeal to you) and ones that you know your child likes. A chosen activity could be sitting together to read, cook, go for a walk, do a puzzle, play cards etc.

NB: We strongly recommend that your activity includes playing, as this is something that we don't usually do enough of with our children. You need to remember to let your child 'lead you' in the game that they chose. And don't get too competitive!

Also, try not to associate One-on-one Time with shopping as your child may link it to material gain, which is not the point of your connection.

2. Give empathy and validate their feelings

We often discount our children's feelings without even realizing we are doing it. For example, if our six year old forgets her ballet bag or his soccer gear and is distraught about it, we might say, "Come on, you don't need to worry about a ballet bag/soccer gear, we'll get it tomorrow," failing to realize that what she/he might hear is that her/his feelings aren't important and have been discounted. It is much more effective to focus on 'connecting' with our distressed child by using empathy to acknowledge their feelings, rather than feel we have to fix things.

Expressing empathy for the emotion they are experiencing (e.g. "You seem sad to have forgotten your ballet bag" or "You seem to be really annoyed to have missed your shot at the goal") allows them to know that we are 'tuned in' to them. By 'meeting them where they are' (instead of where we'd like them to be), we allow them to move on from their upset much faster, and it allows us to then offer help in 'redirecting' their emotion. And when we validate our children's feelings it also allows them to learn how to deal with those emotions, as well as trust themselves and their reactions.

Trusting in yourself in this way is an essential component of self-esteem, so as well as strengthening your connection with them you are also equipping them with the confidence they need to thrive.

This empathy can be demonstrated both verbally and non-verbally to your child, through such actions as sitting next to your son or daughter and giving them undivided attention, or by just hugging them, which often works wonders.

At times, it may be hard to express empathy, especially when we 'know' that our children are making more of a scene than the situation deserves. We need to realize that this is our judgment of the situation, and even if it doesn't seem important to us, it is to them. The more they feel heard, the more we can assist them to recover from their emotion and the less likely our children will feel the need to overreact in the future.

We may also think that giving them empathy in these circumstances may reinforce their behavior. Yet children need to have their feelings accepted and respected for them to be able to self-regulate their emotions.

We also need to be aware that any judgment we make of a child's perception is our own and may not correspond to the way he or she thinks or feels at all. It is really important that we give our children enough space to contradict us and tell us what they're really feeling.

Why it works

When we give empathy to our children and validate their feelings, they feel listened to and understood. When they come to us expressing sadness or other feelings, it is usually because they crave connection with us, and the best way we can meet their need is by showing them empathy rather than discounting their feelings.

This sense of being heard teaches them in turn how to show empathy towards others, and how to show it towards themselves – a gift for life! When children hear their feelings being validated they are better able to deal with them and are able to 'come out' of difficult states of emotion far quicker, rather than be 'stuck' inside them. When a child is able to understand the difference between their (temporary) emotions and their underlying (permanent) self, they are given the skills to process, rather than be dominated by, an emotion or feeling.

How to give empathy and validate their feelings

1. **Don't deny your child his or her feelings or try to save them from it**: don't tell your child: "It's going to be ok" or "Come on, it's not that bad!" or "Calm down."

2. **Do not immediately ask your child "Why are you crying?"**, even if you have no idea why they are in such emotional distress. Much of the time children find it hard to answer this question, and asking it of them doesn't help them process their emotion. If you really need to because your child is not shar-

ing the reason, you can ask this after following the steps below.

3. **Meet them 'where they are' by acknowledging your child's feelings and help name their feelings**: Your child may not be able to understand, acknowledge or explain the emotion they are experiencing, therefore you can help them by reading the signs of their emotional state by observing their behavior and body language (just as one might look for the tell-tale signs of tiredness). This includes 'negative' emotions such as anger or sadness. Helping them put a name on their emotions enables them to 'own' this feeling, and therefore control it. Words are not only empowering, but they also 'normalize' situations, turning them from an unknown, amorphous mass into something knowable and manageable[15]. For example:

   a. **When your child is upset and throwing a tantrum**: "You seem really frustrated and angry," or "You seem to have a lot of trouble coping with what I just told you?"

---

[15] Gottman, John, *Raising an Emotionally Intelligent Child*

b. **When your child has hurt themselves**: "Oh, this must hurt!" or "You seem in a lot of pain, the fall must have been harder than it looked?"

c. **When your child is getting very angry with their sibling**: "I can see that this situation is upsetting you."

d. **When your child is confiding in you**: encourage them with Active Listening.

e. **When your child is misbehaving**: always start by giving them empathy and then apply consequences.

4. **Help your child redirect their emotions (only once you have done the above)**. When your children are younger, a good way to do this is to put them in 'thinking mode':

a. **When your child is upset and throwing a tantrum, you can give them a choice. For example**: "Would you like to come with me to your room and play a game or stay here on the floor?"

b. **When your child has hurt themselves**: "Do you need help getting up or can you do it by yourself?" or "Does this hurt a lot, average or just a bit?" or "Would a hug make you feel better?"

c. **When your child is upset with their sibling**: "Fighting won't solve the situation, if I were you, I would try using words instead."

d. **In most other situations, you can ask your child**: "Is there something that I can do to help?"

e. **Give them a hug**: keep in mind that giving our children hugs is an essential way to redirect their emotions and to demonstrate our love to them – some psychologists go as far as saying that we need to give a minimum of 12 hugs a day to our children for them to thrive.

NB: The more you practice the above, the faster your child will be able to deal with their emotions. It is therefore really worth taking the extra time to help children process their emotions from an early age, as you will both reap the benefits later.

Also worth noting is that as your child grows older (we would say from the age of seven), they are in a better position to understand their feelings, and it can be better not to make an assumption about what they're feeling. Instead, you can start making more general statements rather than try to name their feelings, such as "Seems like you are having strong emotions, do you want to talk about it?".

3. Organize family meetings

Family meetings are an invaluable tool for family (re) connection and for encouraging our children to cooperate once they are four years or older. These regular get-togethers (usually weekly) make every family member feel that their needs are important and are a great setting to teach good values. Family meetings encourage children to be involved in the decision-making side of family life, as well as teaching them to take responsibility for setting their own rules, including deciding the consequences of breaking these rules, all of which helps to boost their confidence in their abilities and raise their self-esteem.

Family meetings should ideally include the whole family, so make sure you invite even the youngest of siblings to join you, giving them an activity, such as drawing if they are too little to participate in the discussion side of things. The benefits of sitting down together and discussing how the family should work together are enormous. Most of all, a family meeting allows our children to feel a sense of belonging and responsibility at being 'in touch' with other family members.

Why this works

Family meetings create a great opportunity for each family member to communicate and express their needs, and to help find solutions to both their own problems and the rest of the family's. These meetings create a real sense of family unity and teach children invaluable life skills such as showing gratitude, appreciating others, expressing one's needs, sharing responsibilities and solving problems. Most importantly, everyone is given an opportunity to be heard by all, which is invaluable.

How to hold Family Meetings

1. Schedule in (ideally) one family meeting every week. During this meeting, everyone should sit together and switch off their phones and other electronic devices. Children younger than four might not formally participate in the meeting as it is harder for them to have this kind of longer discussion. But they should ideally sit down next to the rest of the family and can occupy themselves by drawing or some other activity that will not disturb the meeting.

2. Elect two family members to act as Chairperson and Secretary.

The role of the Chair is to lead the meeting to make sure that the agenda is covered and everyone gets to speak.

The role of the Secretary is to take the meeting notes so that there is a record of decisions made during the meeting. Younger family members may need help with this. Although, this step may make it sound 'too serious,' it provides a good structure and children will look forward to the day when they will be allowed to be Chair and/or Secretary (once they grow older and/or have more experience of participating in Family Meetings).

3. Open the meeting with compliments and gratitude. Each person should take a turn addressing every family member to express gratitude or give a compliment. Siblings will usually find it difficult to express gratitude and give compliments to each other, so we have to first model this behavior ourselves – they will usually become more comfortable doing it after a few Family Meetings.

4. Ask every family member to share a moment that they have been proud of since the last meeting.

5. Go through the 'Agenda,' which may include one or more of the following:

- Individual issues: each family member has the opportunity to raise their need or identify a problem they may be experiencing.

- Hold a Problem-Solving session (see Chapter Five) to deal with family challenges.

- Decide on a chore system: allocate tasks and household duties.

- Plan activities and family fun days.

- At the end of the meeting, do something fun as a family that is age-appropriate (e.g. play a board game, or 'I went to the market and bought...').

- It may sound a bit cheesy, but it adds to the sense of bonding to end the meeting with a family hug!

4. Repair to keep the connection

Many of the things we do when we 'lose control,' such as yelling, getting angry, shaming with words, using any kind of physical aggression, etc. create a disconnection between our children and ourselves and can damage their self-esteem. Losing connection with our children is a sad loss.

As we explored earlier in the book, children crave connection, which is directly related to their self-esteem, but it is also our connection with them that makes them want to behave well. So it is essential that we 'repair' the conflict or outburst wherever possible, thereby restoring the connection and removing their fear of being punished.

Children are just learning to be emotionally mature, and it is therefore unrealistic to expect them to instigate making amends (although they sometimes do, particularly if they've been coached to do it). If we try to force them to say sorry when they don't feel sorry, we are merely encouraging them to lie just for the sake of our getting an apology. Far better to first offer the apology ourselves. In other words, if we want our children to say sorry and mean it, we need to model it by saying sorry first.

We can then each take responsibility for our actions and even discuss what we could do differently the next time around.

Why this works

Connection with our children, rather than the use of power, should lie at the heart of our influence 'over' them, because it is what makes them want to behave appropriately. It is therefore essential, that both you and your child are able to address and repair any misunderstandings, outbursts and any kind of conflict before they do any lasting damage. Reparation of this kind is not only essential to their self-esteem, it also acts as a foundation for better levels of trust, communication and connection between you, both now and in the future.

How to Repair

1. You can apologize to your child straight after an incident if you have lost your temper or done something that you immediately regretted. However, we're talking here about how to 'repair' the relationship beyond this initial apology. This is particularly useful if you are like some 'strict' parents who find it difficult to apologize when they haven't managed to calm down yet.

2. Sit down with your child once you're both calm (this can be several hours after the incident) and apologize for what happened.

3. Present them with your version of the facts, ideally using an 'I feel' message. e.g. "When you were arguing so much, I felt disappointed and angry."

4. Make sure that you tell your child the things you regret about your own behavior and stress that this is not the best way to react in these situations. Often by this point, your child will be apologizing themselves, taking responsibility for what they did

and hugging you (but don't despair if they don't as this can sometimes take time!).

5. Let your child share their view of the event and make them feel that you have understood their point of view by actively listening to them. For example, "So you felt that I was ignoring you?".

6. (Optional step): you can finish with a problem-solving session (see Chapter Five) to define what you could both do to prevent this from happening again. If you do this, make sure that you're not putting all the responsibility on your child, it's important that you find ideas of what you could do differently as well.

7. (Optional step): Children need to be reminded that their parent's love is unconditional, even if we sometimes overreact (and maybe even scare them a bit). From time to time, it's important to remind them that we still love them just as much as we ever did, regardless of the circumstances.

5. Teamwork

As parents, partners or caregivers, it's almost impossible to agree on every aspect of parenting. Our attitude towards our children and family is formed as much by our individual characters and temperaments as it is the result of our past experiences, including how we were parented ourselves. Our levels of tolerance to 'mis'behavior, noise levels, a child's cry and all the many other things that we will experience with our children are informed far more by our 'reflexes' than by rational, strategic thinking – however much we might aspire to the latter.

Given these differences, it's not surprising that we can disagree with our co-parent as to how to deal with our children. But arguing about how to deal with our children can make them confused as to which instruction they should be following. Unsurprisingly, it can also have a negative impact on their self-esteem if they're receiving mixed messages about their behavior. Fortunately, there are relatively easy ways to adapt our parenting styles so that they positively complement one another, to the benefit of our children's self-esteem, confidence and the connection they have with us.

Our partner/co-parent most probably loves our child as much as we do and he/she is most likely doing what he/she thinks is best for them. We therefore, need to take a tolerant approach towards our partner's parenting skills, and try to manage our differences without resorting to blame, 'guilt trips' or other forms of negative judgment.

The reality is that once we have adopted a tolerant, rather than intransigent, attitude to our co-parent we are likely to discover that their parenting style is far more able to complement our own than we once believed. And having entered into a new spirit of understanding, we are far more likely to work as a fully functioning and effective team. Being aware of the strengths and weaknesses of each parenting style means avoiding the good cop/bad cop stereotypes, which children can so easily exploit.

It is also important to have realistic expectations of ourselves, our children and our partner so that we don't chase the fantasy of becoming the 'perfect parent.'

In order to become a better team, we need to learn to resist the impulse to intervene when we don't agree with the way our partner is reacting to a situation, even if we're just trying to be supportive. The fact is that when we interfere with our co-partner's parenting, we are sending the following messages to our child: "Your mother/father is not doing a good job of handling you, so I'll have to do it." While the message to our partner can be interpreted as: "Honey, since you don't have the necessary parenting skills, I'll take care of this."

The best way to help under these sorts of circumstances is to step back (leave the room if needed), and allow your partner to prove that he or she has what it takes to handle the situation without you 'coming to the rescue.'

Why this works

Parenting is the ultimate teamwork and requires a lot of tolerance, particularly if both parents are equally involved. Conflict between parents can create anxiety in children and they will tend to take advantage of the 'rifts,' which will in turn create even more conflict between parents. It is therefore important to show a united front even when parents have different parenting styles. Consistency (in one's own parenting style) also helps children have a clearer understanding of what is expected of them.

How to have good teamwork

1. Start by having a conversation with your spouse/ partner or co-parent in which you discuss:

    a. What your hopes are for your children and what you want them to become.

    b. What your default parenting styles are likely to be. Do you tend to be more lenient or more strict?

c. Agree with your partner what your 'core' values are, for example, good manners, tidiness or spending quality family time together.

d. Then decide what you both consider to be acceptable and unacceptable behavior based on these principles. This enables you to set household rules that are clear and accepted by everyone.

e. The above exercise is likely to leave areas where you might disagree, and this is fine as it is almost impossible to reach an agreement on everything. You will need to both agree to be flexible in these instances and be accepting of these differences.

2. Make an agreement with your partner, that so long as you are both maintaining these shared values and rules, you will allow each other room to express your individual parenting styles and you will stop blaming each other for your weaknesses.

3. If there are tensions surrounding certain household tasks (bedtime routine, bath time etc.), then divide them. Agree on 'territories' that you will each need to commit to respecting. The key thing is to both play to your strengths, thereby reducing friction

simply by agreeing on the tasks you will each do and ensuring that you stick to the plan.

4. Don't compensate for your spouse's parenting style. So for example, if your spouse has a more lenient approach to parenting, be aware that you will probably have a tendency to compensate by becoming stricter, and this will only serve to undermine their authority and make them feel unsupported.

5. Avoid taking sides with your child and/or sabotaging your partner's actions, and don't allow your child to manipulate you into conflict with your partner. For example if a child says, "But Mom/Dad always lets me stay up late!" (most kids will try this at some point or another!), answer, "He/She may well do, but right now I'm the one who's responsible for looking after you." And for single parents, try adapting this answer slightly by saying: "I hear that your mom/dad may do things differently, but in this house, this is how we do things." Children need to learn that there may be different sets of rules in different environments and they are usually ok with it as long as we are consistent.

6. It is important to try to be as consistent as possible when it comes to applying these techniques and

whatever parenting strategy agreed upon with your partner. Consistency is difficult, because as human beings it is in our nature to have moments where we just want to relax and not have to give too much thought to our actions or behavior. However, it's always important to ensure that you send a clear message to your child so they know where the boundaries are and don't get confused by mixed messages.

7. If and when you disagree with your partners' reactions to your child's misbehavior, avoid intervening or expressing this in front of your child because otherwise you send the message to your co-parent that they are incapable of dealing with the situation. If you feel your partner is starting to lose their temper and think there may be a better way to deal with the situation, try asking, "Can I help?". However, if their answer is "No," then do respect this.

8. If you find it too difficult not to intervene, and particularly if you are getting angry, it's much better to remove yourself from the situation by leaving the room rather than allowing the disagreement to escalate. Otherwise, children will sense the tension

and this can have quite a detrimental effect on their wellbeing.

9. If you feel the issue is still unresolved, discuss this with your partner later on when your child isn't present. This may involve talking about how you could have handled things differently and identifying how to deal with the situation in a more effective way, should it arise again.

10. Model conflict resolution: sometimes despite our best intentions, we can find ourselves disagreeing and arguing with our spouse in front of our children. In an ideal world, find an amicable solution in their presence, so they learn how to deal with conflict rather than fear it. This is also important because if children don't see the resolution they could be left with a sense of anxiety about what has happened. However, if there is too much tension to resolve things, it is better to agree to discuss this later – either one of you can leave the room if necessary – rather than let the argument flare up.

11. Think about your children's relationships with other caregivers such as relatives, child-minders and nannies. Clarifying your wishes and expectations to these other caregivers and sharing some of the skills/techniques in this book will help prevent

them from inadvertently undermining your efforts when you're not around. However, while consistency between different caregivers makes things easier, it is not a requisite because children understand that different people will treat them in different ways. As long as both parents are as consistent in their approach as possible, then it doesn't matter quite so much if other caregivers do things differently.

12. Finally, make sure that you celebrate your partner for improvements in how he/she is dealing with your child – even if they seem insignificant to you – and show appreciation for the effort they are making. This is the best way to get rid of blame and make this a positive self-reinforcing cycle.

6. Real life example – Using Emotion coaching to develop self-esteem and resilience

My daughters and I love to play games together, and we particularly like playing a card game that tests the speed of your reactions. It's like the card game 'Snap,' but a little more challenging, which makes it great for playing with older children.

One afternoon, three of us were playing this game, and I was winning more often than my youngest daughter, Yara. It was clear that Yara was getting upset by this, even though she was beating her sister, Noor, who's five years older than she is!

When I won again for the third time in a row, Yara started to cry.

I was annoyed by this and told her so, "Why are you getting so upset? We're here to play, not win. You might be losing to me, but you're still beating your older sister. Now get your act together!".

Unsurprisingly, this caused the situation to escalate, and she started to cry even louder. I was frustrated with her at this point, so I decided that we should stop playing to prevent things from escalating any further.

Later that day, after I'd had time to think, I realized that I hadn't dealt with the situation very well. After all, she was only seven years old, and I needed to coach her to better manage her emotions, rather than expect her to know how to always be able to process what can be quite overwhelming feelings.

So, I closed my eyes and focused on trying to visualize how I could handle the situation better. In my visualization, instead of getting frustrated with her and putting an end to the game, I tried connecting with her by using empathy instead, and then giving her some ideas on how she could better deal with these situations.

Luckily, I didn't have long to wait before I got an opportunity to see if my visualization had been useful. Because the next day, we decided to give it another shot and to all play again. And, sure enough, we found ourselves in the exact same scenario. Yara was beating her older sister, but losing to me, and when she lost to me for the third time in a row, she burst into tears.

But this time, instead of getting annoyed and dismissing her feelings, I said, "I can see that losing again is making you really upset." And then I paused to allow her to process this and feel the empathy. I then added "It must be frustrating to find yourself in the same situation as yesterday?".

She slowly stopped crying, and I could see that she was starting to think about what I'd said, so I continued, "Do you know that some parents let their children win?". She managed to stop sobbing and looked at me curiously and answered: "Yes I know."

So I then added: "Would you like me to let you win?" By this point, her brain was fully engaged in 'thinking mode,' and she was looking at me with a half smile on her face. After a moment of thought, she smiled and answered, "No, because it wouldn't be fair for me to win like that, and I wouldn't learn from it."

I was so proud of her answer because she'd managed to not only process her feelings but also realize that it's ok to be frustrated because she can learn from it! I had faith in her ability to be mature enough to work the issue out by herself, but I was still surprised by quite how mature my seven-year-old daughter had proven herself to be.

I was so happy that I'd used empathy to connect with her instead of getting annoyed like I had before, otherwise this moment would never have happened!

The key part of this is that using empathy to connect with Yara meant that she felt listened to and understood. Once she could see that I was acknowledging and accepting the way she felt, she could start to process and understand the emotions she was experiencing without being over-whelmed by them.

And by giving Yara the opportunity to prove to me, but most importantly to herself, that she had the maturity to find a solution on her own strengthened our relationship. It clearly also raised Yara's confidence and self-esteem, and increased her ability to handle challenging situations.

Chapter 7

Key Life Skills to Develop in Children

"A pessimist sees the difficulty in every opportunity, an optimist sees the opportunity in every difficulty."
Winston Churchill

It is important to help children develop their metacognition (the awareness and understanding of their own thinking process) and learn how their thoughts affect their feelings and behavior. So, as explained in the Introduction, we've created a series of illustrated journals called the Happy Confident Me Journals.

Through 10 weeks of daily journaling, with explanations of key concepts such as the growth mindset, mindfulness, the power of positive thinking, etc., these journals enable children to gain a better understanding of the way their mind and emotions work, helps them develop key life skills, and equips them with a toolkit so they can meet life's challenges head on.

In the following pages we have given an explanation of the key skills that our children need to learn, and we've included excerpts from the Happy Confident Me Super Journal. Many of these concepts have already been explained in the previous chapters, but the objective of this chapter is to focus on the ones that are relevant to your children and help you explain these sometimes complex concepts to them in a way they'll understand. The language used is aimed at children aged 7 to 12.

1. Helping your child to become more self-aware

Our level of self-awareness significantly influences the way we feel and behave and how we perceive ourselves. It is a key component of confidence and self-esteem because it increases your child's ability to understand what they are good at and to be realistic about what they can achieve.

If a child has little self-awareness, they are more likely to be indecisive, often find it hard to express themselves and tend to feel insecure and uncertain about who they are and what they're capable of.

So, if you'd like to build your child's confidence, raise their self-esteem and make them more resilient, one of the most effective ways of achieving this is by focusing on developing their self-awareness first.

How to explain this to kids (excerpt from our Super Journal)

Knowing Yourself

Knowing ourselves really well (also known as having strong 'self-awareness') is something that the World Health Organization lists as one of the 10 most important life skills that we humans need.

So, if you don't know yourself very well, it's time to learn how fabulous, interesting and unique you really are! Think about things like what your superpower might be, what your dream pet could be like, and all the little things in life that make you smile.

Learning about ourselves

Overall, our self-awareness can have a real effect on how we feel and behave, each day.

When I don't know myself very well:	When I know myself:
Quite often I feel uncertain, and insecure about myself.	I often feel comfortable and confident about myself.

Sometimes I get confused about what I want to do.	I can make exciting plans because I know what I love doing.
When I get stuck or upset, I can feel like that for ages and don't know how to feel better	When I get stuck or upset, I know what to do to feel better.
It's difficult to talk about or understand how I feel.	It's easier to find the words to talk about how I feel.

2. Understanding and coping better with feelings

Children need to feel unconditionally loved and supported by their parents.

In order to properly fulfill this role, we need to be able to help our kids identify what they're feeling. And the first step in doing this is by acknowledging their emotions, even if we think they're silly, trivial or exaggerated.

As explored earlier in the book, we often undermine or dismiss our children's expression of their vulnerabilities, particularly when we are trying to help them overcome a painful emotion or experience, without even knowing we are doing it.

Whilst our intentions are undoubtedly well meaning, when a child hears expressions like "Don't worry, it's not so bad" or "There's no need to cry" they are likely to feel dispossessed of the right to feel that particular emotion.

By first acknowledging and then helping our children identify the emotions they are experiencing, not only tells them that it is ok for them to have that response, but that they should be able to trust their feelings in the future, too. And once they feel reassured and empowered in this way, children become more receptive to our suggestions as to how to improve the situation.

How to explain this to kids (excerpt from our Super Journal)

In just one day we have LOADS of different feelings… we could feel relaxed, angry, bored, happy, worried and surprised at different times.

It can really help you feel better when you can identify all of your different feelings.

"What am I feeling?"

Some feelings are easy to recognize, when we're really happy we smile, we laugh, we feel super-relaxed or excited. When we feel yucky, it can be harder to recognize what sort of yucky we're feeling – hard to name that emotion or even talk about it.

Are we angry, frustrated, sad or upset? It takes LOADS OF PRACTICE to understand and tune in to our feelings and work out what they are.

Why does it matter?

But hang on, who cares if you don't know *exactly* what you're feeling? Do you really NEED to know? Well, you definitely do. It's the harder feelings that are actually the most important to be able to name and talk about! Because if you can understand and name them, you can work out how to feel better.

- If you understand what's going on inside, you feel calmer

- If you find words to talk about your feelings, your friends and family can help you

- If you can work out what you need, you'll find it easier to come out of the yucky feelings

If you get to know the kinds of things that usually make you feel sad, or angry, or worried you won't get taken by surprise, and you'll know better how to handle it.

Noticing and writing about your feelings:

The cool thing is that noticing your feelings and then writing and drawing about them is a *brilliant* way to get to know what you are feeling.

A useful hint to get to know what you feel, is to notice where you feel it in your body…Yes…that's where we feel our feelings!

For example: Have you ever had 'butterflies' in your tummy when you're nervous, or tight fists when you're angry, or a headache when you are worried or overwhelmed, or been heavy all over when you are sad? We all feel our feelings a bit differently in our bodies. So, start to notice where YOU feel your feelings.

When you make a note of how you feel each day, it's like turning a key! You unlock this knowledge about yourself and discover how to feel better!

3. Teaching the importance of Positive Thinking and Gratitude

A lot of research has been done recently on positive thinking and gratitude.

This research shows that thinking positively creates positive feelings, which leads to more positive actions and behavior and ultimately therefore, more happiness and success because of the 'positive loop' created.

And other research shows that simply by focusing on just three things that we're grateful for every evening can significantly increase our level of happiness, and this works at any age!

On the other hand, negative thinking often causes feelings of inferiority, anxiety and self-doubt and presents us from seeing all the good things we have in our lives, and children are no exception.

So it's crucial to help children focus on the positives and encourage them to show gratitude as often as possible because it is one of the key aspects of developing their happiness, confidence and self-esteem.

How to explain this to kids (excerpt from our Super Journal)

Positive Thinking and Gratitude

We want you to be as happy and as confident as you can be. Did you know that one of the most powerful things that affect this is how you think and how you feel?

AND did you know that how you think and feel is very connected to how you behave?

Put simply…

What you **think** ⇨ What you **feel** ⇨ What you **do!**

There's quite a lot going on in these human bodies and minds of ours, all the time – our thoughts creating feelings, (and even feelings creating thoughts).

To be more happy and confident, you need to pay attention to HOW you think. When you TAKE CHARGE of your thinking, you'll enjoy better outcomes.

Helpful, positive thoughts ⇨ Good feelings ⇨ Making better choices

Understanding Positive and Negative Thoughts

So, what's the difference between a positive or helpful thought and its opposite – a negative or unhelpful thought?

Unhelpful thoughts tend to create horrid feelings – feeling sad, hopeless, wobbly or angry and frustrated.

But helpful thoughts tend to make us feel the opposite – confident, stronger, calm and happier – like anything is possible!

Good feelings help you make different choices, because you are generally MORE POSITIVE. You will...

- Learn more new things and be able to enjoy and celebrate your successes.

- Worry less about making mistakes and enjoy learning from them.

  Push forward and keep going even when something is tough.

- Be able to help your friends when they need it, and make new friends too!

4. Developing a Growth Mindset in Children

As we explained at length earlier in the book, there are practical steps that we can take as parents to help ensure that our kids develop a growth mindset and maximize their chances of reaching their full potential.

As we discussed in Chapter Two, our ability to learn new skills and get better at them through practice, effort and perseverance is called neuroplasticity. Much like a muscle in the body will get stronger through repeated use, the brain gets 'stronger' in the exact same way by forging and strengthening neural pathways in the brain.

How to explain this to kids (excerpt from our Super Journal)

Building your Growth Mindset

Do you know what a 'growth mindset' is?

It's very cool…

In the 'olden days,' before scientists and doctors knew that much about our minds or brains, we all believed that when we were born, the things that we could do brilliantly were completely fixed for our whole lives.

So, whether you were a math whizz, good at French or incredible at art or soccer, that was just part of who you were.

But now, scientists have found out that THAT'S NOT TRUE and our brains can change and grow – depending on how we use them.

So really, we have a lot of power – a superpower even – the power to be good at ANYTHING that we want to!!

The science bit

- Every time you think the same thing or do the same thing, a 'neural pathway' is created in your brain.

- The more times you do it, or think it, the stronger and faster the pathway becomes.

- When scientists take special photos (like x-rays) of brains they can actually see these pathways light up!

What does that mean for you?

- When you learn and practice new things, you'll get new pathways, and build stronger pathways.

- As each pathway gets stronger, the things you're doing will get easier and easier and you'll get quicker and better at it!

Why having a Growth Mindset is AMAZING

If you're learning something new and finding it difficult, it's not because you 'can't' do it, it's just that you haven't practiced enough yet!

This is really EMPOWERING. You can get better at anything you put your mind to.

- If you feel you're not good at something, just use the word 'yet' to keep your growth mindset, for example 'I am not good at math YET.'

YET is your SUPERPOWER word, use it often and just see how much more powerful you feel!

5. Mistakes as Opportunities for Learning

Earlier in the book, we explored how the way in which a child perceives the mistakes they make plays a major role in whether they develop a fixed mindset.

The key thing to remember is that by demonstrating (through our actions as well as our words) that it is ok to make mistakes, we can help our children to learn how to embrace their mistakes and develop a growth mindset.

How to explain this to kids (excerpt from our Super Journal)

Making Mistakes

Have you noticed that when you learn something new, you nearly always have to 'get it wrong' quite a few times before you get it right? (Like falling off your bike!)

Sometimes, when we keep making mistakes, we might even want to just give up – we feel so stuck, frustrated and annoyed. It's a horrible feeling – and we've all had it!

On a 'bad day' we might even believe we aren't good or clever enough. But that's not true!! Remember, it's normal to doubt ourselves sometimes, but we don't have to feel bad, because making mistakes is actually perfectly normal – in fact it's essential.

We're all good enough and we CAN do it – just not YET.

It takes practice! Remember learning about Growth Mindset? We actually HAVE to make mistakes – sometimes lots of them – on our way to learning something new. It's how our brains grow!

So we haven't failed, we're just stuck, or we've hit a bump on the road to success…

There's no such thing as failure

If you ever think that you've 'failed' – or made a mistake – it is actually just your…

First

Attempt

In

Learning

When you keep going and trying, making mistakes is a good sign. It means your brain is busy making new pathways. So, it's proof that you're stretching yourself – really growing.

If you only ever did the easy things, you'd never get a stronger brain or be able to do new things – how boring! Loads of famous people have made HUGE mistakes, loads of times, before they got really good at what they are famous for. (Even Walt Disney, Lionel Messi and JK Rowling!)

So, don't let your mistakes get you down – celebrate them and keep going!!

6. Resilience

Resilience is the ability to keep going even when you find things challenging and bounce back from difficult situations, and it empowers children to be able to embrace mistakes, take on new challenges and thrive in any situation. It is an essential tool that helps kids navigate their way through life's inevitable challenges.

That's why it's essential to give your children age-appropriate challenges, as this will help them to develop their own problem-solving skills and nurture their sense of responsibility and resilience.

How to explain this to kids (excerpt from our Super Journal)

Bouncing Back

Sometimes things are difficult to learn, and we make mistakes. When that happens, how do we push through and keep going?! How do we remember about our Growth Mindset, and allow ourselves to keep growing?

When we hit a block, it can sometimes be hard to carry on. When we do find the oomph to keep going and keep practicing, we call it 'bouncing back.' And the ability to find our own 'oomph' is called perseverance!

Remember when you learned to ride a bike, swim, skateboard or ice skate? Did you jump in, jump on, and whizz off like a pro?

Most likely you bumbled and fumbled, shouted, cried and got frustrated. Did you want to give up sometimes? That's normal!

But if you can swim or ride a bike now, you actually did keep going, until you could do it, because you were determined to get there – you persevered. That meant you could bounce back from those difficult moments.

To be able to persevere like that, it's really important to remind yourself that in the end, you WILL be able to do it!

Bouncing back is also called being 'resilient.' The more resilient you get, the better you feel. You recover more quickly when you find something hard and can keep practicing until you really enjoy it!

Remember: You are good enough, and by persevering and being determined to keep going whenever you feel stuck, you'll end up feeling really proud of yourself

Little by little, you'll get closer to being good at whatever it is you want to be – a cyclist, mathematician, soccer player, artist, doctor or anything else!

7. Teaching Mindfulness

Mindfulness is the simple practice of bringing our attention back to what's happening in the here and now. It helps kids gain a better understanding of why they react to certain situations in the way they do, how emotions affect them and what they can do to bring their attention back to the present moment.

When we focus on the present moment, we find it much easier to think clearly and manage our emotions, which is why mindfulness is such an effective way of reducing anxiety and promoting happiness, in both adults and children alike.

Thanks to neuroplasticity, our brains are constantly developing throughout our lives, but our brains are developing at their fastest rate during childhood. Mindfulness promotes skills that are controlled by the prefrontal cortex, like concentration and cognition. So, teaching kids mindfulness from as early an age as possible is a great way of helping them develop essential skills like self-regulation, self-care and patience.

How to explain this to kids (excerpt from our Super Journal)

Being Mindful

To keep your body healthy you eat well, get some exercise, brush your teeth, and get enough sleep. But what about your mind?

Did you know that you need to keep your mind healthy too? After all, it's in charge of everything you think, and how you feel!

A healthy mind has positive, helpful thoughts so we can feel good more of the time.

One way to keep your mind healthy is to be 'mindful.' This means focusing your mind on NOW – not thinking about yesterday or tomorrow, just this moment.

When our brain is too busy we can get all stuck because of so many thoughts buzzing around. Sometimes these thoughts are unhelpful, like if we're anxious about something that hasn't even happened yet, or are feeling worried about something that we did yesterday.

It can be really unhelpful, annoying and make you feel bad. It can stop you from concentrating, or enjoying what you are doing, and sometimes stop you falling sleep.

Has that ever happened to you?

Turning Down the Volume

So, wouldn't it be great to have a magic button to switch your mind off, or turn down the volume, when it's too busy with unhelpful stuff?

Well no one's invented a magic button yet, but you CAN switch your mind into being calmer, slower and 'mindful.'

Being Mindful

By learning to relax and breathe slowly, you can practice meditating. This helps keep your brain healthy and you can CHOOSE the thoughts that you have. This will help you to make more out of each day and to think more clearly.

Learning to meditate and be mindful just takes a bit of practice.

1. Relax

2. Breathe slowly and focus on your breathing

3. And slowly quieten down your head

In just a few minutes, you can slow your brain down, relax and choose what it is you want to think about. It just takes practice.

8. Empathy, Kindness and Validation

Research shows that when we are kind to others, this stimulates our brain's production of serotonin and oxytocin, and the same is true for the person we show empathy and kindness to. These hormones help us to feel calmer, more relaxed and less anxious. So, if everybody were to be a little kinder and more empathetic to one another, the world would be a better and happier place.

This is a great way of explaining the power of empathy and the importance of kindness to our kids, but the most powerful way of getting the message across is through our actions and behavior rather than words alone.

We should try to look for opportunities in daily life to model empathy and kindness, and the best place to start is by being kind and empathetic with our children, even when we don't agree with them or struggle to understand their feelings.

And when children are given empathy, they feel listened to and understood, which makes it far more likely that they will show kindness and understanding to those around them, so it's a win-win!

How to explain this to kids (excerpt from our Super Journal)

Kindness and Empathy

Is it important to be kind?

We're guessing your parents have taught you that it is – do you know why? And do you agree?

Well, it is incredibly important because when we are kind, we make other people happy!

So, what is kindness?

In the dictionary it says it's being friendly, generous and considerate – ways we make someone else feel good by how we behave.

And as well as actions – it is an attitude, an expression, a look, a touch – anything that lifts another person.

So – we know that being kind makes other people feel good. But what about you, how does being kind make you feel?

Did you know?

Research shows that even if you only do one act of kindness a day, you will feel:

- Happier
- Healthier
- Less stressed
- Less anxious

That's because being kind floods your brain and body with happy hormones* that make us feel calmer, loving and loved.

*The scientific name of these feel-good hormones are serotonin and oxytocin

Kindness is Contagious

When people see someone being helpful and kind, they also are flooded with the same happy hormones – they feel good, so are more likely to be kind to others too!

Do you ever think about how other people are feeling?

This is called EMPATHY, and it's also linked to kindness.

When you practice empathy it helps you work out what act of kindness might be the best one for the important people in your life. Empathy comes from listening when your friends talk to you and trying to imagine how they might be feeling. It also helps us understand how we might be affecting other people with our behavior – what we do, or how we talk to them. Will it make them sad or happy? Showing empathy will really help you show more kindness and receive more too!

Can you think of different acts of kindness that you could do each day? Here are some examples…why don't you think of some more?

- Hold a door open for somebody
- Help your parents with a chore (before they ask you!)
- Say something nice to a friend who looks sad

Acts of kindness can spread across your community, your town, a city or even the world! It all starts with one person, and that person can be you!

9. Self-Acceptance

Teaching your children to love and accept themselves can take time and effort, but it's one of the most important things you can do for them as it's vital for their happiness and wellbeing. And one of the most effective ways of doing this is by finding ways to show them that you love them unconditionally and convey to them that they are 'good enough' just as they are – even if we'd like them to improve on so many levels because we want the best for them!

Of course, everyone's journey to self-acceptance is different, but the following excerpt has some great tips for teaching kids the importance of accepting themselves for who you they are and loving themselves unconditionally.

How to explain this to kids (excerpt from our Super Journal)

Accepting Yourself

In your journal so far, you have read and written all about knowing yourself and boosting your confidence…and we hope you're starting to feel proud of yourself, and more confident!

Now, we want to share a secret:

Did you know that right now, exactly as you are, without doing ANYTHING at all, you are actually – JUST RIGHT?

That's right. You are 'perfectly imperfect,' exactly as you are right now.

You don't have to be 'the best' at anything or even have yet found a special thing you love doing…

Yes, you can CHOOSE to learn more, to practice new things…to be more kind…or to persevere. These things will definitely make your life more fun and challenging…

…but whatever you are practicing, however many things you are, or aren't yet feeling confident about…you are ALREADY good enough just as you are.

You are no better or worse, no more or less important than any of your friends. Or in fact than anyone else in the world! We are all equally special. And this is extra-specially important to remember.

We are each completely unique. With our own likes, dislikes, qualities, passions, similarities and differences. And that is just fine.

If you'd like to help your child to develop positive habits of daily journaling about gratitude, and equip them with the essential life skills described in this chapter, it may be worth checking out our Happy Confident Me Journals on www.happyconfident.com.

Conclusion

As we've seen, self-esteem and confidence are key to happiness and success and there are many ways in which we can help to develop these traits in our children. Being aware of the impact that our words and actions have upon our child's personal development and their sense of self is an essential part of this process. We also need to be aware of the most common parenting mistakes so we can avoid making them and prevent our children from adopting a fixed mindset.

Because although there is no such thing as a 'perfect parent,' there are steps that each one of us can take to become more effective in our approach to parenting and equip our children with all the tools they need to be able to thrive.

Of course, there will still be difficulties and challenges along the way, but never despair. There are countless examples of children who appear to dislike school and other forms of learning and may be labeled as lazy and not 'capable' by their teachers and others, but who still go on to achieve great things in life, which is well illustrated by Dominic O'Brien's story shared in the Introduction.

We must remember that as parents, one of the most important jobs we have is to show our children that we will always believe in them, no matter what. When we allow our children to make affordable mistakes and they see that we have faith in their ability to survive hurt, upset and disappointment, they start to develop more faith in themselves. And when we empower our children to believe in themselves, we also empower them to become happy and independent adults. So when spending time with your children, keep some of the key tools shared in this book in mind:

- Show children how to celebrate their mistakes by embracing yours as this will help make them more resilient and will increase their willingness to take on new challenges.

- Refrain from rescuing them from difficult experiences and unpleasant emotions – this will help train their 'disappointment muscles' and better prepares them for the realities of adult life.

- Help them to see that in every difficulty or challenge they face lies an opportunity for learning and growth.

- Always focus on the effort and progress your child has made when participating in a task, exam or activity rather than the outcome as this will help them to develop a growth mindset and the art of self-motivation.

- Be selective and honest in the praise that you give, and remember to ask them questions to help them self-evaluate (such as "You must be proud of yourself given all the efforts you've put into this,") before giving your own 'judgment' and praise.

If you are consistent in the application of the tools in this book, you can maximize the chances that your children will one day – hopefully sooner rather than later – develop a growth mindset, find their passion(s) and become completely responsible for their own success.

We hope you enjoyed this book! To find more articles and tools as well as child-centered activities and quizzes to develop your child's happiness and self-esteem, visit www.happyconfident.com.

Resources and Further Reading

Aldort, Naomi, *Raising our Children, Raising Ourselves*, Book Publishers Network, 2005

Bronson, Po and Merryman, Ashley, *Nurture Shock*, Ebury Press, 2009

Biddulph, Steve, *Raising Boys, Harper* Thorsons, 2010

Cohen, Lawrence, *Playful Parenting*, Ballantine Books, 2012

Dreikurs, Rudolf, *Children: The Challenge*, First Plume Printing, 1990

Dweck, Carol, *Mindset: The New Psychology of Success*, Ballantine Books, 2007

Faber, Adele and Mazlish, Elaine, *How to Talk so Kids Will Listen and Listen so Kids Will Talk*, Avon Books, 1999

Faber, Adele and Mazlish, Elaine, *Siblings Without Rivalry*, Piccadilly Press, 1999

Fay, Jim and Cline, Foster, *Parenting with Love and Logic*, Navpress, 2006

Fay, Jim and Charles, *Love and Logic Magic for Early Childhood*, Love and Logic, 2000

Gordon, Thomas, *Parent Effectiveness Training*, Three River Press, 2000

Goleman, Daniel, *Emotional Intelligence: Why it Can Matter More Than IQ*, Bloomsbury, 1996

Gottman, John, *Raising an Emotionally Intelligent Child*, Simon and Chuster, 1997

Ginott, Haim, *Between Parent and Child*, Crown Publications, 2004

Hawn, Goldie, *10 Mindful minutes*, Piatkus, 2011

James, Oliver, *They F*** You Up: How to Survive Family Life*, Bloomsbury, 2006

James, Oliver, *How not to f*** them up*, Vermillion, 2011

Kennedy-Moore, Eileen, *Kid Confidence*, New Harbinger, 2019

Kohn, Alfie, *Unconditional Parenting*, Atria Books, 2005

Kohn, Alfie, *Punished by Rewards*, Houghton Mifflin, 2000

Markham, Laura, *Peaceful Parent, Happy Kids*, Penguin Books, 2012

Medina, John, *Brain Rules - 12 principles for surviving and thriving at work, home and school*, Pear Press, 2014

Mischel, Walter, *The Marshmallow Test: Mastering Self-control*, Little Brown and Company, 2014

Nelsen, Jane, *Positive Discipline*, Ballantine Books, 2013

Nelsen, Jane and Lott, Lynn, and Glen, Stephen, *A-Z*, Three Rivers Press, 2007

Mc Cready, Amy, *If I Have To Tell You One More Time*, Penguin, 2012

Palmer, Sue, *Toxic Childhood*, Orion Books, 2007

Palmer, Sue, *Detoxing Childhood*, Orion Books, 2008

Reivich, Karen and Shatte, Andrew, *The Resilience Factor*, Three Rivers Press, 2002

Sanders, Matthew, *Every Parent*, Penguin Books, 2004

Shefali Tsabary, *The Conscious Parent: Transforming Ourselves, Empowering Our Children*, Namaste Publishing, 2010

Siegel, Daniel, *Parenting From the Inside Out*, Jeremy P. Tarcher, 2003

Siegel, Daniel, *The Whole Brain Child*, Bantam, 2012

Stoll Lillard, Angeline, *Montessori - The science behind the genius*, Oxford University Press, 2007

Webster-Stratton, *The Incredible Years*, Incredible Years, 2005

www.ingramcontent.com/pod-product-compliance
Lightning Source LLC
Chambersburg PA
CBHW071459070426
42452CB00041B/1926